SELECTED POEMS
by
ARTHUR DAVISON FICKE

Books by
ARTHUR DAVISON FICKE

FROM THE ISLES, 1907

THE HAPPY PRINCESS, 1907

THE EARTH PASSION, 1908

THE BREAKING OF BONDS, 1910

TWELVE JAPANESE PAINTERS, 1913

MR. FAUST, 1913

SONNETS OF A PORTRAIT-PAINTER, 1914

CHATS ON JAPANESE PRINTS, 1915

THE MAN ON THE HILLTOP, 1915

SPECTRA (WITH WITTER BYNNER), 1916

AN APRIL ELEGY, 1917

MR. FAUST, ACTING VERSION, 1922

SONNETS OF A PORTRAIT-PAINTER, AND OTHER SONNETS, 1922

OUT OF SILENCE, 1924

SELECTED POEMS

With a Preface on the Nature of Poetry

BY

ARTHUR DAVISON FICKE

NEW YORK
GEORGE H. DORAN COMPANY

CONTENTS

CONTENTS

[x]

SELECTED POEMS

Nocturne in a Library

I

Books on the tables—books along each wall—
Books in proud bindings—torn books in a heap—
Some books content with century-hallowed sleep,
And others that on quiet midnights call
Until they wake me from my dreams, and hale
Me shivering down to listen to their story,
While stars go by in unregarded glory,
And dawn comes up, cold and estranged and
      pale. . . .
O long-time friends! What other power than you
Can nourish our old passion?—hold us true
To the young faith which once our hearts avowed?
When in the solitude of the evening light
We keep your quiet vigil with the night,
You bring the sun. The day brings back a cloud.

Here where the lamplit room's book-guarded space
Is all the world, and not an alien breath
Enters to this small citadel,—this vast place
Where dead men's voices break the hush of death,—
Here through the night-hours I turn well-loved
    pages
That in my youth seemed eloquent of a plan
Divined by eager poets, confident sages,
Of the great destiny and high worth of man.
Still the tall spires of their heroic vision
Rise clear before me, as they did of old.
And yet a savage laughter of derision
Jangles now in my heart. The night grows cold.
Soon the first pallor will tremble in the sky—
And then, I know, these midnight dreams must die.

Like the recurrence of an old despair,
Dawn soon will turn the windows slowly grey.
Yesterday whirled our hopes like leaves in the air;
Now comes the chill wind of another day.
Yesterday whirled us in the tempest-boast
Of wars that saved a world for liberty:
Today dawns tragic, now that we have lost
Even our faith we had an enemy.
Today looks in through the blank window-pane
Upon the dreaming dupes that late we were,
And whispers—"What the world endured, was
    vain;
In vain the high hearts found their sepulcher
By a certain river, or in a certain wood.
I rise, a new day, flushed with future blood!"

[14]

Cruel and evil and aloof and cold
This dawn confronts us. For with secret breath
New war-lords like the ones we saw of old
Today, in council, still are whispering death.
Again they weave their intricacies of hate
Which, on some other dawn, inevitably
Shall be the arbiters of the young men's fate—
Shall be the swift tornado from the sky.
In every land is raised the old device
Of greed and terror, ignorance and hate.
That which we swore should never happen twice
Grows strong,—without our gate, within our gate.
And high-and-low and near-and-far conspire
To heap the rich fuel, and invoke the fire.

II

I will not look at this. . . . I will return
To my calm lamplight; and, as years ago,
Take down the sacred volumes—slowly turn
The nobly singing pages that I know:—
Listen again while the young Shelley's voice
Speaks beautiful madness, better than our truth.
Upon his sunlit peaks, I will rejoice
In the unlimited eager hopes of youth.
Or I will watch the ghost of Goethe move
Through its vast dream-world, where is still a place
For liberal human hope, and generous love,
And the slow-gathering wisdoms of the race—
And live his golden days, and feel his trust
That life is more than wind whirling the dust.

III

Yet—I put down the volumes. . . . There is gone
The god that in these pages once we found.
Too swift, too pitiless has our fate whirled on
That we turn back to that once-holy ground.
No magic can restore, ever again,
The confident promise of those earlier years.
For we have seen the very sunlight wane,
And watched our world go down in blood and tears.
Towers of our spirit crumbled in their pride
When century-carved cathedrals fell in flame.
A hope of ours died where each soldier died;
And we endured all of each nation's shame.—
Shame, for the race of which we were a part
That held such treachery in its secret heart.

And so, tonight, seeing the hopes that fail,
Seeing the brute that is a part of man,
I think that Galahad and his Holy Grail
Had best make way for some less gilded plan.
We, lewd and savage cousins of the ape,
May well cease boasting of our family tree,
And with a certain modesty try to shape
A dream more consonant with reality. . . .
—As a poor madman, guessing that his brain
Inherits some defect of fatal blood,
Accepts the curse of an accursèd strain,
And halts, midway in his grandiloquent mood—
And for one honest hour, ceases to boast
His lordship of that forest where he is lost!

IV

We, the so-doubtful heroes of today—
We children of all irony, all despair,—
We proud explorers who have missed our way—
We, Icarus-brood hurled headlong through the
    air,—
For us, what guide and leader can suffice?
What champion or what prophet or what sage?
What herald of an Earthly Paradise?
What golden hero from the Golden Age?
Who—save the ancient, tattered, unhorsed knight—
The renowned windmill-warrior, sore and spent—
That luckless champion who in every fight
Proved his cause lost beyond all argument.
Yes! deck the lean horse! Bring the rusty lance!—
And let Don Quixote ride forth toward romance!

See how he rides, that battered ancient shade—
(Our hero, or else hero have we none—)
Don Quixote, vanquished, and by fate betrayed,
The sorriest scarecrow underneath the sun:
See how he rides! Indomitable still,
With Roland's horn still echoing in his breast—
Spending the riches of his knightly will
On causes vain, and hussies sore-distressed—
Careering through a world that has no place
For the quaint chivalry that the legends told—
Seeing brass basins turn to helms of gold—
Finding the Virgin in the harlot's face:
The dupe of an archaic lying vision—
Time's fool . . . the ages' jest . . . the oaf's
    derision. . . .

O dauntless hero of the rusty mail!
You knew the appalling truth before you died—
Knew that your knighthood was of no avail,
And that the old romancers all had lied.
Yet shall your followers, to the farthest age,
Still saddle the lean horse and grasp the lance,
And seek your dusty highroads of romance,
And your vain wars against the giants wage.
For comedy is in our deepest blood;
We breathe frustration from the very air.
O great Don Quixote! Let your reckless mood
Still be our light, through midnights of despair—
That we, though knowing all that once you knew,
Hopeless and grim, adventure forth with you!

V

When all our troubled errantries are done,
And faiths and lures alike have lost their sway,
And but the subtle body, rotting alone,
Is left to prove the daring of our day;
And if we won, head-high, or if we lost
Is now no matter anywhere; and unswerved
The seasons roll, indifferent to the cost
Of pageantries we ruled or faiths we served—
Then of the passion whose attainment was
So serious business while we lived and sought,
Perhaps some faint and ghostly flush shall pass
Out of a vase or song or tower we wrought,
And rest one moment upon men as blind
As we were, bent on hopes we leave behind.

I trust the young—who, dreaming, shall awake
On sudden Springs and capture, fluttering by,
These gleams of memory—capture them, and make
Old lights to flicker on new wings that fly.
Then such a dreamer shall, in one, bear fruit
Of all that from our million Junes could live,—
From pulses quenched, lips even whose dust is mute,
Hopes whose so mighty part was fugitive.
He shall inherit us; and not yet come
Into the full enthrallment of his day,
Shall feel, within his bosom, stir the bloom
Of all our Springs, a thousand years away—
The moment's mirror of our final light
In infinite dust vanishing down the night.

So out of horrors that could break the heart,
Did the heart keep its bitterer memories,
There desperately survives some rarer part—
Old, meager consolations such as these.
And when the baffled spirit dares to brood
Alone with its own destiny face to face
It finds, in that grim midnight solitude,
Some ancient smouldering altar of the race.
With hard-won fuel we feed the little fire,
Shielding its hesitant flame against the blast—
We, heritors of an unfulfilled desire
That it burn brighter than in the somber past.
At midnight, by the ghostly flame, alone,
We pray,—beside that altar's blood-drenched stone.

Lyrics

BONDWOMAN

Across an ancient darkness
I see your figure move,
Too proud for my compassion,
Too separate for love,
Aloof and calm and lonely,
Intent on ways apart;
While I—perhaps I only—
Questioned your heart.

Your heart despised its station,
Too human, hence accursed.
As of some fatal nation
The sacrifice, you durst
Disclose to no man ever
The pulse that gave you wings.
And you soared upward never
From your shadowings.

From shadows you departed
Toward shadows none can know,
You the high eager-hearted.
But now when May-nights blow

Their separate and lonely
Low winds out of the west
I think of you, you only,
And your locked breast.

Gone:—and it shall not matter.
The doom lies on the race.
Earth like a glass must shatter.
What of one vanished face?
Nothing is worth the loving.
Nothing has aim or end.
Yet tonight my heart is roving
Lonely, my friend.

FATHERS AND SONS

Child to whom my loneliness
Cries—and cries, I know, in vain—
Down the years I look and bless;
Down the years, let my hand press
Strong your shoulder. I am fain
You should reap from my sown pain
Flowers of joy and loveliness,
Child I love, and love in vain.

You will never turn to me
As I turn and cry to you.
Regions strange and visions new
Shall be yours to search and see.
Old and alien I shall be.
I who love you set you free.
Yet recall I cried to you,
Child I love so utterly.

PORTRAIT OF AN OLD WOMAN

She limps with halting painful pace—
Stops—wavers—and creeps on again—
Peers up with dim and questioning face
Void of desire or doubt or pain.

Her cheeks hang grey in waxen folds
Wherein there stirs no blood at all.
A hand like bundled cornstalks holds
The tatters of a faded shawl.

Where was a breast, sunk bones she clasps.
A knot jerks where were woman-hips.
A ropy throat sends writhing gasps
Up to the tight line of her lips.

Here strong the city's pomp is poured . . .
She stands, unhuman, bleak, aghast,
An empty temple of the Lord
From which the jocund Lord has passed.

He has builded Him another house
Whenceforth His flame, renewed and bright,
Shines stark upon these withered brows
Abandoned to the final night.

THE THREE SISTERS

Gone are the three, those sisters rare
With wonder-lips and eyes ashine.
One was wise and one was fair
And one was mine.

Ye mourners, weave for the sleeping hair
Of only two your ivy vine.
For one was wise and one was fair,
But one was mine.

THE GREY RIVER

The swallows have departed.
The harvest moon has come.
O rare, O lyric-hearted,
Why are you dumb?

Your words, that once in summer
Glowed like a magic wine,
Are frozen.   Aye! and dumber
Than yours are mine.

The mists upon the river
Drift like ghosts in a dream.
I think such greyness never
Has hung on the stream.

I think such greyness never
Has brooded over me.
Greyly flows the river
Down to the sea.

A WATTEAU MELODY

Oh let me take your lily hand,
And where the secret star-beams shine
Draw near, to see and understand
Pierrot and Columbine.

Around the fountains, in the dew,
Where afternoon melts into night,
With gracious mirth their gracious crew
Entice the shy birds of delight.

Of motley dress and maskèd face,
Of sparkling unrevealing eyes,
They track in gentle aimless chase
The moment as it flies.

Their delicate beribboned rout,
Gallant and fair, of light intent,
Weaves through the shadows in and out
With infinite artful merriment.

.   .   .   .

Dear lady of the lily hand,
Do then our stars so clearly shine
That we, who do not understand,
May mock Pierrot and Columbine?

Beyond this garden-grove I see
The wise, the noble, and the brave
In ultimate futility
Go down into the grave.

And all they dreamed and all they sought,
Crumbled and ashen grown, departs;
And is as if they had not wrought
These works with blood from out their hearts.

The nations fall, the faiths decay,
The great philosophies go by—
And life lies bare, some bitter day,
A charnel that affronts the sky.

The wise, the noble, and the brave—
They saw and solved, as we must see
And solve, the universal grave,
The ultimate futility.

.   .   .   .   .   .

Look! where beyond the garden-pool
A Venus rises in the grove,
More suave, more debonair, more cool
Than ever burned with Paphian love.

'Twas here the delicate ribboned rout
Of gallants and the fair ones went
Among the shadows in and out
With infinite artful merriment.

Then let me take your lily hand,
And let us tread, where star-beams shine,
A dance; and be, and understand,
Pierrot and Columbine.

TO THE HARPIES

You who with birch or laurel
Are swift to scourge or bless—
Silence your foolish quarrel
Before her loveliness.

What though she went a-travel
Down paths you do not know?
Your words shall not unravel
Webs that allured her so.

Hush now your foolish babble
Around her golden head.
Shut out the prying rabble.
Be happy.   She is dead.

Now give one final kindness
That late you dreamed not of—
Silence, to cloak your blindness—
Peace, since you know not love.

ATTIC

Firelight danced along the uneven walls.
The rooms forgot that they were old and dank.
They caught the music of your light foot-falls,
They echoed with our laughter and our calls,
They blessed the food we ate, the wine we drank—

And they grew human, tender, sweet, and wise.
We loved them as we loved each other, then.
Now they are part of fading memories
As I forget your hands, your breast, your eyes . . .
But I can love no other home again.

TO A CHILD—TWENTY YEARS HENCE

You shall remember dimly,
Through mists of far-away,
Her whom, our lips set grimly,
We carried forth today.

But when in days hereafter
Unfolding time shall bring
Knowledge of love and laughter
And trust and triumphing—

Then from some face the fairest,
From some most joyous breast,
Garner what there is rarest
And happiest and best—

The youth, the light, the rapture
Of eager April grace—
And in that sweetness, capture
Your mother's far-off face.

And all the mists shall perish
That have between you moved.
You shall see her we cherish;
And love, as we have loved.

THE ORACLE

I lay upon the summer grass.
A gold-haired sunny child came by,
And looked at me, as loath to pass,
With questions in her lingering eye.

She stopped and wavered, then drew near
And bent her gay attentive head,
And o'er my shoulder stooped to peer.
"Why do you read?" she said.

"I read a poet of old time,
Who sang through all his living hours
Beauty of earth—the streams, the flowers,
And stars, more lovely than his rhyme.

"And now I read him, since men go
Forgetful of these sweetest things;
Since he and I love brooks that flow,
And dawns, and bees, and flash of wings."

She stared at me with laughing look,
Then clasped her hands upon my knees:
"How strange to read it in a book!
I could have shown you all of these!"

ON HAVING KNOWN AN ASTRONOMER

I think some constancy was his
Of worlds that move from ours apart,
Hushing with deeper harmonies
The rioting passions of the heart.

Though darkness brooded on the way
Wherein his measured course was run,
He dwelt in a serener day
With movements of a greater sun.

And we who knew him came to know
Some touch of that high silent grace
Which let no clouded tempest blow
The calming starlight from his face.

No intimate dream can give release
From life's enforced and narrow bars;
Yet was there in that bosom's peace
Something not sundered from his stars.

TO THE BELOVED OF ONE DEAD

The sunlight shall not easily seem fair
To you again,
Knowing the hand that once amid your hair
Could stray so maddeningly,
Now listlessly
Is beaten into mire by summer rain.

The spirit has its sanctities in death—
But the bright clay
Knows naught of recompense. And the swift breath
That in some darkened place
Once swept your face—
What shall sublime that memory away?

He died amid the thunders of great war;
His glory cries
Even now across the lands; perhaps his star
Will shine forever . . .
But for you, never
His wild white body and his thirsting eyes.

THE GOLDEN SWALLOW

I heard a maiden singing
Down a valley, in the sun—
"April is beginning!
I see the small leaves springing!
And the winter's done!"

I saw a golden swallow
Fly up out of the south.
The sunlight seemed to follow
Where he touched hill and hollow
With a gold leaf in his mouth.

Today new green will cover
Each scar of winter ills.
The night-bird has gone over.
The loved turns to her lover,
And light sweeps the hills!

TRYST

I

Midnight comes, keeping
A two unsleeping.
Darkness gravely covers
Two laughing lovers.

II

Grey light slowly
Enters dimly stealing
Into their dazed holy
Hush—revealing
Drowsily their sea-deep.
Above them thunder
The waves of day
Muffled and far away.
To them, their sleep
Is only deep-sea wonder.

III

Down their coral caves
Hearing distant waves,
Light they think they know
As a thing of long-ago;
Day itself can seem
But a paler dream.

LEGEND

I do not love you, no, nor all your beauty,
Nor have I terror of your delicate magics;
I love only the silence that around you
Makes a low twilight.

Yet I desire that thunderous storms of passion
For all I am, should surge and clamor through
     you—
Scattering your follies and your delicate secrets—
Shaking your twilight.—

That like a temple-bell across the darkness
I should forever echo in your spirit,
With tones of legend and of high disaster
Haunting your silence.

SONG COMPOSED IN A DREAM

I built me a house, with a mountain above,
A stream and a willow, a bird and a love.

The mountain was high.   The stream it was fleet.
The willow was gentle.   The bird-song was sweet.

The love she was dark-eyed, and snowy her
    breast.
And she was my joy, and my dusk, and my rest.

SEA-SKETCH

Sand, sand, long white sand.
Foam on the water, snow on the land.

Grey, empty, homeless sky,
And three bleak gulls flapping by.

You and I, hand in hand
On that edge of sea and sand.

You and I, dazed as though
Life had died an age ago.

[37]

DAY-DREAM

A pale girl, naked,
On a black-maned horse
Rides, by a foaming
Water-course:
With forests behind her,
Silent and black;
She lifts no finger,
She looks not back.
But onward, onward,
A slender ghost,
Rides; and in shadows
Again is lost.

LONG AND LOVELY

Long and lovely, cool and white,
She lay beside me all the night.

Long and lovely, hushed and warm,
She touched me, thigh and breast and arm.

My body was one tremulous sense
Of her slight body's eloquence.

I was a drowned man, in the sea
Of her immaculate melody.

Drifting slowly down to sleep,
I longed to laugh, I feared to weep.

While hushed and lovely, cool and white,
She lay beside me all the night.

THE MOST BEAUTIFUL

What is so beautiful as the bodies of lovers,
Seeing each other unashamed and naked,
And knowing that not sunrise and not moonrise
Has ever touched the world with such a wonder?

What is so living as the embrace of lovers
Who in the darkness turn and clasp each other,
And laugh, and feel their souls and bodies shaken
By the wild passion of discovered beauty?

What is so silent as the sleep of lovers
Who, when their longing and their love is over,
Shall lie in the dim earth, nor hear the murmur
Of other lovers passionate in the midnight?

QUARTER-MOON OVER ROCKS AND SEA

Savage grey moon going down the west—
Roaring waves on the rocks at my feet—
Heart inscrutable in my breast—
Here for an hour we meet.

The moon sinks slowly through distant veils,
Fading, paling into a haze
As the quiet flood of the mist prevails
Over its flame of memorial days.

And the waves die down as night consumes
Their passion by unresisting peace.
Before the dawn shall their fierce white plumes
Droop in the glassy tide, and cease.

I alone, I alone,
While the sea grows quiet as sea-washed stone,
While the moon turns dark as a burned-out coal,
I alone keep my soul.

Sonnets

SEA MIDNIGHT

Wakeful, I pace the deck and watch the stars
That also have no kinship unto rest—
I who am wounded by those greater wars
That storm across the spaces of the breast.
There is no sweetness that could stay me now,
And yet I long for some unnamèd sweet;
I could not be assuaged by any vow—
And yet I burn to track your flying feet
Toward some last refuge where you shall confess
Something to still me.   What can that thing be? . . .
God, Thou hast dazed me with a loveliness
Ever my own to seek, never to see.
And Thou hast stooped to poison with sure trust
In perfect beauty this poor swirl of dust!

LOVERS' DUSK

Spring fills the air today; with different sound
The whistles blow, out in the foggy bay;
There is a thawing in the sodden ground;
And flowers whose birth is still two months away
Send down the air premonitory ghosts
Of what shall be their odors. As we lie
Here in our dusk of silence, all things lost
Seem phantoms of a winter soon to die.
Nothing is dead that had the power to live;
Nothing can end except what should not be;
Beauty, that far-sought April fugitive,
Comes home to those who trust felicity;
Moments that have the whole of life to give
Pause thus by lovers' couches, tenderly.

DEMAND

Give to me something to be wholly mine—
Something in which no other can have part—
Something no future moment of your art
Can match or hide or cancel or malign.
You have loved others; you will love again.
In time's wide spaciousness, I can only be
A moment's flash of sun-glow through the rain,
A candle-light dim in your memory.
But I must still go onward down my days
With ghosts of you haunting the day and night;
I must endure my knowledge of your ways
Of lovely wantonness and swift delight.
Dear, give me something, now before we part,
Not to be given again. . . . Give me your heart.

POSSESSION

I would possess you with that certitude
Which is the high prerogative of Death—
Subdue to one fixed mood your many a mood,
Catch in one song your many a hurrying breath,
Make of your dear diversity such a whole
So welded that you never might again
Retrieve your rainbow brokenness of soul,
But must my white eternal dawn remain.
And I would do such violence to you, dear,
As only Death, corrupting Death, can do:
Bury your body, to have you always near,
And stop your heart, to keep it ever true,
And hide you in such darkness of embrace
That none, not even I, could see your face.

LEAF-MOVEMENT

From its thin branch high in the autumn wind
The yellow leaf now sails in upward flight—
Hovers at top-slope— then, a whirling bright
Eddy of motion, sinks. The storm behind
With gusts and veering tyrannies would uphold
Even as it downward beats this gorgeous thing
Which like an angel's lost and shattered wing
Across the grey sky sweeps its broken gold.
Another eddy, desperate or in mirth,
Brings it to rest here on the crackled earth
Where men can see it better than on the bough.
What quite preposterous irony of wind's-will
Touches it where it lies, golden and still,
And once more vainly lifts it heavenward now!

HER HANDS

"My hands were loved of many, when I was
young,
Not for the beauty of the flesh alone.
They were as quivering harp-strings that had sung
A music that at last became my own.
Their slenderness was eloquent of blood
Seeking a joy not ever manifest.
My lips and eyes never betrayed my mood
As they did.   And my lovers from my breast
Sometimes have turned to kiss these hands again
That were to me a perfidy and no prize.
Is happiness so small a thing—? and pain
So great a splendor to the lover's eyes?—
Could they not love my joyousness, but only
My hands— that are so terrible, so lonely?"

PORTRAIT OF A STRANGER

She was so young, it seemed that Spring had
    turned
Earthward to make her before brooks were clear
Of their last ice—before first blades appear
Of grass, and not one April flower had burned
Its little light under the pale blue sky.
She was so young, I knew she could not know
Anything more than that the wind can blow
Dark violet-blooms to sway most delicately.
But one calm evening, when a quiet star
Was great and luminous above the west,
We talked of what is good and bad and best,
And how the nearest things are the most far,
And how the things-that-are-not chiefly are . . .
I think, now, Spring's old self lives in her breast.

MARCIA

Marcia! . . . Across the glassy twilit pool
I heard your following playmates call your name.
The pale mists parted, and I saw your cool
Delicate figure poise, and like a flame
Shoot out to the dark water, and emerge
Dripping, silent, and smiling, where I stood.
You turned again and leaping from the verge
Swam toward the darkness, leaving me to brood
All evening on your slender arms and hands,
Your shadowy breast, your swiftly flushing face . . .
Some light still glimmers on these somber lands
Where beauty has one moment left its trace . . .
Marcia! . . . some day your lover shall possess
More of you—but no more of loveliness.

RUTH

Your pale Egyptian eyelids used to stir
Faintly with laughter when I brought a jest.
You were mysterious as a sepulcher
To my young eyes; and that perhaps was best:
For a dim secret, none too good to know,
Must even then have had its dwelling-place
In your still bosom.   I could come and go
Yet never read the silence of your face.
Then on a day the spirit in that tomb
Grew faint, and madness curtained up your eyes
With film on film of desolated gloom
Through which the soul I knew gave no replies—
Until that dawn of strange November rain
When you lay dead, and were yourself again.

LONG AGO

Like him whose spirit in the blaze of noon
Still keeps the memory of one secret star
That in the dusk of a remembered June
Thrilled the strange hour with beauty from afar—
And perilous spells of twilight snare his heart,
And wistful moods his common thoughts subdue,
And life seethes by him utterly apart—
Last night I dreamed, today I dream, of you.
Gleams downward strike; bright bubbles upward
    hover
Through the charmed air; far sea-winds cool my
    brow.
Invisible lips tell me I shall discover
Today a temple, a mystery, a vow . . .
The cycle rounds: only the false seems true:
Last night I dreamed, today I dream, of you.

OLD WIVES' TALE

I saw my grandmother's shadow on the wall
In firelight; it danced with queer grimaces
As if her serious soul were making faces
At me, or life, or God, or at us all.
And I, an urchin lying at her feet,
Then caught my first glimpse of the secret powers
That stir beneath this universe of ours,
Making a witches' carnival when they meet.
Across the firelit dusk my sensitive mood
Dreamed out to mingle with the waifs of time,
Whose unsolved stories haunt the poets' rhyme,
And in dark streets of ancient cities brood
Like sudden ghosts rising above the grime
With premonition of terror that chills the blood.

GIRL BESIDE POOL

I

GO

Trouble not this dark pool! In shallower waters
Go dip the splendor of your naked feet.
Above this surface other of love's daughters
Have bent, and found the mirrored picture sweet—
And smiling down on the reflected face
Have turned, and with a lightened spirit gone
To seek their kindred in a sunnier place.
Why do you, only, dare to linger on?
Why do you, only, with mysterious eyes
Look thus into the pool, where far beneath
The daylit world a lonely darkness lies?
Why do you draw a sudden tremulous breath,
And let the girdle and the robe slip down
As though to plumb the secret depths—or drown?

II

STAY

This is a pool whereof the legends are
Lurid, antique, doubtful, and numerous.
To this brink you have wandered from afar
Imagining it as thus, or thus, or thus.
What do you seek—a silence clear to lave
Limbs that are tired of frothy mountain-streams?
Or do you grope toward the terrific wave
That swept the girlhood of your secret dreams? . . .
The girdle falls; unbound is the bright hair,
And the pale feet are pausing by the flood . . .
There is a solemn hush upon the air
As golden evening, in heroic mood,
Scatters, before the night's immense despair,
Its glow on the dubious pool of this dim wood.

A GREAT LADY FROM THE NORTH

Those were odd tales you told me when I was
  young
And used to sit in wonder at your knee.
They had the northland horror and mystery—
Come down, I think, from ages when songs were
  sung
Beside a fire in some cold vaulted hall
For bearded men who smelt of beef and mead,
Who, chin on fist, gave heed as children heed,
While torches smoked and spears leaned by the wall.
Their world was yours; my elders and my betters
Perplexed me with their wisdom and their pride,
Being far too eager that I should learn my letters.
But you, blood-curdling kitchen-queen, swung wide
Awful romance for me, and burst my fetters
With lovely murder as I dreamed at your side.

HOLY WRIT

It does not seem so many years ago,
Those nights when I lay shivering in my bed
And saw the candle-light bless my aunt's head
With its celestial sanctifying glow,
And heard her read strange story after story
Of Jonah, Adam, Moses, Esau, Ruth—
Of Solomon's old age and David's youth—
Things haunting, tender, terrible, or gory.
Still can I see the Queen of Sheba's hair;
And all real lions are but mockery
To him who once knew Daniel's; there's no tree
That can with Eve's great Paradise Tree compare:
A golden light gleamed through that ancient air
That leaves me homesick in modernity.

DOCTOR OF BUTTERFLIES

His white beard tossing in the wind of speed
Made by his passage, down the dusty road
He disappeared, giving no slightest heed
To us his nephews who so bravely strode
After him.   In his gentle giant hand
He brandished as he went a little net . . .
Dear titan uncle from an alien land,
I see you always thus: I see you yet,
With laughing bearded mouth and serious eyes
Pursuing the mirages of your dream—
Most learned Doctor of the Butterflies—
Most childlike follower of wings that gleam!
Now you are dead. . . . Surely above your tomb
Some butterfly hovers against the gloom.

THE OLD MIDWIFE

Her old face bent to me and tried to peer
Through the thick mists blindness and time had
    made
To circle her with their perpetual shade
Beyond the sunlight of the mortal year.
And then she mumbled—"No, I do not know you!"
And turned, as if enraged by some cruel jest.
"Try, try again!" I said, "you half have guessed;
Trace with your hand my face, and it will show
    you."
She touched my face with that dry withered hand;
And a vague shudder I could not understand
Swept me with sense of my own death hovering
    nigh. . . .
For hers had been the first touch on this earth
To meet me when in the flickering hour of birth
I drew my faint breath, and there was an I.

MOMENTS FROM THE LOST YEARS

I

MARCH FIFTH, 1916

These are the thunders; soon upon the crest
Of a fierce earthquake-wave shall we be whirled.
Prophetic darkness haunts today my breast
And terrible shadows seem to fill the world.
I see each friend go down in the wild foam—
Some dead in battle, of whose fate shall come
The thrilling whisper of high courage home;
And others vanished, and their record dumb;
And others turned to maimed distorted things
Returning hideous who went forth in grace;
And all my land blackened beneath the wings
Of a red Horror with a vulture's face;
And every soul in fierce futility
Lost, though he stay or go, or live or die.

II

FEBRUARY THIRD, 1917

The streets are strange and dizzy is the air.
The cold bites inward; my dazed blood is dumb.
There is a hovering horror everywhere
And the sick sense of all that is to come.
I peer into familiar eyes to find
Tidings in them as in my own of change.
But they are curtained or unmoved or blind.
Dizzier grows the air, the streets more strange.
Yesterday life was prosperous and sure:
Tomorrow—ah, tomorrow we shall be
Motes of a nation summoned to endure
Whirlwind and rocks and overwhelming sea—
Tossing like leaves under a riven sky—
Lost, though we go or stay, or live or die.

III

OCTOBER FIRST, 1918

The incessant tearing shock of sudden guns
Here at my side, and the slow incessant rain,
Daze me with black monotony that benumbs
The fear of death and the keener fear of pain.
Dim, miserable days—will they ever cease?
What if they did—what can it matter now?
We shall not live to see the day of peace
That men will make sometime, somewhere, some
     how—
See ignorant mobs bring their new hates to birth
And celebrate them with the conqueror's drum.
Their secret madness will possess the earth
When the frank madness of the guns is dumb. . . .
If we return, be it with savage mirth
To loathe the thing we fought for, and called home!

Beauty in Exile

It is ordained,—or so Politian said,—
That he who by some dryad-haunted brook
Or silver bathing-pool or secret glade
Shall, wandering in the dusk, suddenly look
Upon a naked goddess at her bath,—
He from that hour leaves happiness behind,
And doomed to all the splendor of her wrath
Returns as did Teiresias, smitten blind:—
Blind to the common and decaying things,
Blind to the dying summer and the dust,
Blind to the crumpled wall, the broken wings,
The yellow leaf, the sword ruined with rust;
Blind, blind to all save the wild memory
Of Beauty naked against a stormy sky.

For Beauty kissed your lips, when they were young,
And touched them with Her fatal triumphing;
And Her old tune that long ago was sung
Beside your cradle haunts you when you sing.
Wherefore there is no light in any face
To win you from these memories as you roam;
Far though you seek, you shall not find a place
Wears the mysterious twilight-glow of home.
You are an exile to those lonely lands
Far out upon the world's forsaken rim
Where there is never touch of meeting hands,—
Always you must go on, through spaces dim,
Seeking a refuge you can never know—
Wild feet that go where none save Beauty's go!

Beauty—what is it? A perfume without name:
A sudden hush where clamor was before:
Across the darkness a faint ghost of flame:
A far sail, seen from a deserted shore.
Out of the dust and terror it can spring
And be, for us, all that there never was:
The sun lives only to illume Her wing
Which rises, hovers, soars, and soon must pass
Into high chaos once again. But now
While She still lingers round us in mad flight
We shall revive the vigor of our vow,
Assured that all our hopeless love was right,
And watch the wings that fade, pale, and are gone,
Knowing that they are life, and they alone.

[63]

In Beauty's name, I love you.   Life's grim story
Is swept with rainbow lights when you draw near.
A singular and inescapable glory
Comes from the sun when thoughts of you are here.
Your presence is not anything, or not much;
But when your dreams come whispering to my doors
I leave my crumbling house,—lift wing,—fly,—
    clutch
Great battlements, and walk legendary floors. . . .
Poor dust! poor ignorant instrument of great
    powers
That through you blow their silver trumpet-cry!
How savage is this destiny of ours
That fashions music out of agony,
And lets us hear, across the iron night,
The wing-beats of each other's lonely flight!

Not till the temples of our secret trust
Are blown in mist across a rainy sky,
And music crumbles wholly into dust,
And carven marbles into silence die—
Not until what we dream and what we know
Are merged and made inseparably the same,
And beauty dead a thousand years ago
Ceases to haunt us with a living flame—
Not till the harvest of slow-ripening Time
Is brought in golden sheaves triumphant home
And planets round into the perfect rhyme
Of death after their million years aroam—
Not until then shall any strangeness move
From its fixed place the strangeness of our love.

[64]

This is the deep security of our love—
The faith that neither, widowed, can survive
To view an earth where dreary pigmies move
Down paths where once the gods were so alive;
For we have made our compact out-of-time
And marked our passion with a fabled date
And had our banns inscribed in druid rhyme:
Unto our feast no guest shall come too late.
There is a music in the upper air
That shall deny to me if you are dead.
A summer wind will whisper in your hair
Though all except the name of me be fled. . . .
Ah, radiance of two spirits one must wear
When in the end the other bows his head!

If you went out of this strange world tonight,—
This world of flesh that is the one I know,—
And joined the legends of our lost delight,
And were as dead as Helen, ages ago,—
It would be a dim world you left behind,
One without reason, and incredible.
I think that I should know how move the blind
Or the doomed souls who grope their way through
        hell.
And yet there is no heaven, to pay for this
Grim possibility that I dare to view.
You dead, I dead,—how would the other miss
The torture that I was, and that was you!
How would the lingerer love the other—when
No one was left to make life mad again!

To us who are beyond all loves and wars,—
To us,—who keep no faithfulness of trust
In anything but sea-winds and wild stars
And horror and a sudden laugh and dust,—
The gifts that can be given are few and rare.
There are no jewels yet mined for me to set
Upon your haunted breast; and for your hair
The seas have made no fitting pearls, as yet.
But you,—one thing be still content to give
Where here I watch the dusks go down in fire:
A love of loving, far and fugitive,—
A faith in beauty and the heart's desire,—
A sudden sense of that which might befall
Could life be nothing and our dreams be all.

I cry to you—and like a windy mist
My words go past you: it is well they do. . . .
Not any kiss that you or I have kissed
Loses or gains from what I bring to you. . . .
Not anything that life has ever told
Has whispered what I come to you to learn.
And a flame whiter than the arctic cold
Is what I speak of when I say—I burn! . .
Go by, image! Go by, immortal dust!
It was your destiny to make manifest
The god again: unfathomable, your trust
Nurtured the deity at a virgin breast,
Holy, and lonely, and immaculate,—
And branded with your fate and with my fate.

[66]

We meet in lands of longing where there are
No jealousies to poison love's bright lips
With faith or with fidelity.   Does a star
Secrete itself in shadows of eclipse
Save for one eye alone?   Or must a wall
Shut in a garden from the general sun
Because one spirit, dearest of them all,
Walks there a dreaming hour when day is done?
Nay, with more certainty of love, we know
Nothing diminishes what is yours and mine;
As richer with all other loves you grow,
The dearer is your wealth that I divine;
All that enchants you is a golden glow—
Ripening the grapes of our communion-wine.

Against mine eyes let your dreams beat their wings
Blindingly bright, as they so long have done.
And let the music that your bosom sings
Sing still to me: it sings to me alone.
Here in the murk and mystery of the earth,
Where strangers wed, and foemen dwell as friends,
And brothers cease their brotherhood at birth,
And who as son begins, as alien ends,—
Here send again those blinding dreams that come
Singing and crying out of your wild heart—
Let them to me, to only me, turn home—
For they are mine,—they are another part
Of my own soul, somehow afar and free—
Till your voice sings them dizzily back to me.

Above the region of eternal snow,
Where on the ultimate icy granite peak
The sun shines always, and there always blow
Clear singing winds,—there might we stand and
    speak
Truly and tenderly. . . . We have moved apart
Ever from the confusions of the earth:
We have been acquiescent, with half a heart,
To those necessities which gave us birth,—
But we have honored or believed them never. . . .
—Is it that we were dream-befooled, or wise?
Were we too dull, or too perversely clever?
Was it conceit or wisdom sealed our eyes? . . .
What we have sought,—is it a quickening light,
Or but the aurora of an Arctic night?

Thanks to our happy fate, we two shall meet
Never more humanly than heretofore.
No enmity of chance shall guide our feet
Down paths of dreaming toward one twilight door.
For in that little room there were no place
For the great promise that we two have made
Of marvelous glow upon each other's face:
We should be lonely there, and half-afraid.
There, if we met, two Titans would arise
Between our breasts, passionate to proclaim
We were but strangers to each other's eyes—
Bleak ghosts without a fragrance or a name—
Pale wicks that sent once a preposterous light
Of lying signal through the hollow night.

In parable alone we speak the truth
And in the interludes of a troubled dream,
On this wide platform between age and youth,
And name as nothing all the things that seem. . . .
—A swamp of violets stretches from our feet
To an horizon violet-hued with dawn.—
And need you say that loveliness is sweet,
Or need I say that all the best is gone? . . .
As actor, liar, prophetess, and child
You cross in curious paths the mortal plain
Where to be virtuous is to be defiled,
Where to be happy is to drown in pain,—
Where home is in the bosom of the wild,—
And to have loved is to have loved in vain.

In times hereafter, when there shall be told,
To light man's legend with heroic glory,
The chronicle of the famous loves of old,
Enriching with their passion life's bleak story,—
Of some shall be recounted sacrifice,
Or courage, or how pitifully they died,
Or what tumultuous madness swept their eyes. . . .
But us let Time remember for our pride.
Let men hereafter know, that never two
Did with serener arrogance bend their glance
Downward upon the human world they knew
And cut the knots of mortal circumstance
And turn to worlds where only shadows move,
Their faces lit with the great pride of their love.

And these shall be an elegy for you,—
These groping syllables out of many years,
Mixed of things felt or dreamed, things false or
    true.
No one shall guess what mockery or tears
Or pitying smiles or dizzy lighted eyes
Between us made communion, or if dumb
Our lips were . . . There are certain destinies
That have a home beyond the mortal home. . . .
But if you should survive me, come, some day,
To where, not knowing anything, I shall lie—
And look down at the stupid mound of clay,
And look up at the splendor of blue sky,—
And know that neither you nor I could know
All that our love meant to us, long ago.

Peculiar ghost!—great and immortal ghost! . . .
How many generations before mine
Have you not haunted? . . . I shall join the host
Of those who, when Proserpina's dark wine
Touches their lips, forget the haze they knew—
The years when—tortured, heaven-dreaming men—
They trusted sleep, the beautiful and true. . . .
We shall forget our need of sleeping, then!
Everything left behind us like a dream
Shall into an ambiguous darkness fade.
Safe, safe at last, beyond the fatal stream,
Upon our brains oblivion shall be laid. . . .
You will be waiting, on that silent shore;
And we shall speak. We never spoke before.

[70]

Sonnets of A Portrait-Painter

A Narrative

I

It needs no maxims drawn from Socrates
To tell me this is madness in my blood.
Nor does what wisdom I have learned from these
Serve to abate my most unreasoned mood.
What would I of you?   What gift could you bring,
That to await you in the common street
Sets all my secret ecstasy awing
Into wild regions of sublime retreat?
And if you come, you will speak common words,
Smiling as quite ten thousand others smile—
And I, poor fool, shall thrill with ghostly chords,
And with a dream my sober sense beguile.
And yet, being mad, I am not mad alone:
Alight you come! . . . That folly dwarfs my own.

II

A thousand walls immure your days,—and yet
What are they all when, of the thousand, one
Has fallen beneath the curious urge and fret
Of you toward me, of me toward you begun?
When the first fell, I shuddered half-aghast;
The second, now a-crumble in my sight,
Predicts less thunder than the fall late past;
And I await the third with clear delight.
Mingled with all the phantoms of my fear
Are lights of utter lure.   Wherefore I choose
To linger watching, though right well I bear
Knowledge that naught's to gain and much to lose,—
And that there is reserved Hell's choicest flame
For pairs of fools who play this silly game.

III

With what apt ceremony, with how much grace
Of delicate wit and interchange of thought,
Do the marked pair approach the end they sought,
Each praising other's soul or book or face;
Yet in the end inevitably move
Toward a goal different than they have professed.
So love recurrently is only love,
And books and brains are less than lips and breast.
All this, I think, is well, Oh, very well!
It keeps us human though we call us wise.
No one, for being kind, has gone to hell;
And as we look into each other's eyes
We read some stories which we do not tell
That make our earth more homelike than the skies.

[72]

IV

Dear fellow-actor of this little stage,
We play the hackneyed parts right merrily,—
Trifle with words drawn from the poet's page,
And match our skill with cool and conscious eye.
All gracious gestures of each shining rôle
Have been the garments of our summer sport. . . .
But now, when ominous thunders shake my soul,
My reason gives of us no high report. . . .
I could not mimic Romeo had I lain
By Juliet's bier in bitter dizzy truth.
Henceforth my mouthings, choked, inept, and vain,
Will lack the light touch fitting amorous youth.
Let fall the mask! Let end the tinseled play!
Ghastly the footlights front this sudden day.

V

Fate, with devoted and incessant care,
Has showered grotesqueness round us day by day.
If we turn grave, a hurdy-gurdy's air
Is sure to rasp across the words we say.
If we stand tense on brink of perilous choices,
'Tis never where Miltonic headlands loom,
But mid the sound of comic-opera voices
Or the cheap blaze of some hair-dresser's room.
Heaven knows what moonlit turrets, hazed in bliss,
Saw Launcelot and night and Guinevere!—
Or from the cliffs of what great sea-abyss
Tristan and Iseult watched their doom draw
      near. . . .
I only know our first impassioned kiss
Was in your cellar, rummaging for beer. . . .

[73]

VI

Why deck yourself with such unholy art
When none of all this beauty is for me?
I have two eyes; also, a living heart
That takes some impress from the things I see.
Wherefore, I say, this cruelty tonight?—
When you came forth in low-cut sweeping dress,
With flaming lips, pale shoulders, eyes alight,—
A cry of youth, a lamp of loveliness!
O what an evil in you has its nest
That my poor writhings should assuage your will!
A serpent coils within your warm white breast
And sucks the nectar of this flower of ill.
Yet . . . when I come, meet me, as thus tonight,—
With flaming lips, pale shoulders, eyes alight!

VII

Your beauty is as timeless as the earth;
All storied women live again in you:—
Yet with some element of later birth,
Some savor strange, some light troubling and new.
You were not possible until today;
For in your soul the risen Celtic wind
Breathes audible; and tragic shadows grey
From dark Norwegian winters tinge your mind.
The pulse of the world's dreamers who have been
Lemans of beauty, and grown faint thereby,—
The fierce unrest of toilers who have seen
Life as a cage of steam-shot agony,—
Have woven round you, in the burning Now,
A lure unknown to Helen's Phidian brow.

VIII

Come forth! for Spring is singing in the boughs
Of every white and tremulous apple-tree.
This is the season of eternal vows;
Yet what are vows that they should solace me?
For on the winds, wild loveliness is crying;
And in all flowers, wild joy its present worth
Proclaims, as from the dying to the dying—
"Seize, clasp your hour of sun upon the earth!"
Then never dream that fire or beauty stays
More than one April moment in its flight
Toward regions where the sea-drift of all days
Sinks in a vast, desireless, lonely night.
O wind from flushing orchards!—give me breath
Of one white hour here on the marge of death!

IX

Did not each poet amorous of old
Plead the sweet pretext of the wingèd time
To urge his lady that she be not cold
To the dissolving master of that rhyme?
I with no new importunings address
One not less proud and beautiful than they
Whose lovers breathed—"Fleet is thy loveliness;
Let not its treasure slip unused away."
Light hearts! Light words! Here in my tran-
    sient Spring
Let them suffice to hide the things unsaid.
No shadow from the lonely deeps I bring.
Nay, I with gayest flowers will wreathe your head.
Here in the sun I put apart from me
Cassandra, Helen, and Persephone.

X

I am in love with high far-seeing places
That look on plains half-sunlight and half-storm,—
In love with hours when from the circling faces
Veils pass, and laughing fellowship glows warm.
You who look on me with grave eyes where rapture
And April love of living burn confessed—
The gods are good! The world lies free to
    capture!
Life has no walls.   O take me to your breast!
Take me,—be with me for a moment's span!—
I am in love with all unveilèd faces.
I seek the wonder at the heart of man;
I would go up to the far-seeing places.
While youth is ours, turn to me for a space
The marvel of your rapture-lighted face!

XI

Ah, life is good! and good thus to behold
From far horizons where their tents are furled
The mighty storms of Being rise, unfold,
Mix, strike, and crash across a shaken world:—
Good to behold their trailing rearguards pass,
And feel the sun renewed its sweetness send
Down to the sparking leaf-blades of the grass,
And watch the drops fall where the branches bend.
I think today I almost were content
To hear some bard life's epic story tell,—
To view the stage through some small curtain-rent,
Mere watcher at this gorgeous spectacle.
But now the curtain lifts:—my soul's swift powers
Rise robed and crowned—for lo! the play is ours.

XII

Take you my brushes, child of light, and lay
Your colors on the canvas as you choose:—
Paint me the soft glow of this crystal day;
My harder touch would grasp them but to lose
The rose-hung veils, the liquid golden flood,—
I who with palette-knife must pry and strain
To wrench from attitude, face, figure, mood,
A living soul and limn its riddle plain.
What need you teachings of my labored art?
The brush will serve your April winsomeness.
Yet . . . rather lay your head upon my heart—
Draw me to you in a supreme caress,—
That one day, as I paint some throat or hair,
Spring's whole delight bloom like a marvel there!

XIII

Joy, like a faun, her beautiful young head
Lifted from out the couches of the grass
Where, but a moment since, pursued you fled;
And smiled to hear your tripping footfall pass.
For two passed by,—into the meadows gleaming
With evening light across an amber stream.
O Sweet! I marvel now, with all our dreaming,
To find the sweetness sweeter than our dream.
Now we return; and Joy amid her grasses
Follows our steps with soft and curious eyes,
Smiling to see, as your light figure passes,
Your hand that in my hand so quiet lies.
Wide laughing light across the fields is shed . . .
Gravely Joy bends her beautiful young head.

XIV

I have seen beauty where light stabs the hills
Gold-shafted through a cloud of rosy stain.
I have known splendor where the summer spills
Its tropic wildness of torrential rain.
I have felt all the free young dominance
Of winds that walk the mountains in delight
To tear the tree-trunks from their rooted stance
And make the gorges thunderous of their might.
The light, the torrents, and the winds, in you
I thought I had perceived to kinship grown.
It was a dream.   Until this hour, I knew
Nothing—nay, nothing all my days have known
Where storm and cloud and sunlight held such part
As when you came, and swept me to your heart.

XV

It was the night, the night of all my dreams.
Across the lofty spaces of that room
You stole; and where the moonlight's silver streams
Cloudily slanted in upon the gloom,
More silver radiance met them where you moved;
And all the beauty of the hazèd west,
Wherein the moon was sinking, lay approved
Because thus lay your pale, slow-curving breast.
I shall remember,—aye, when death must cover
My soul and body with its rayless tide,—
The madness and the peace of that wild lover
Drunken with life's whole wonder at your side.
I shall remember in life's stormiest deep,—
Even as that night I knew you there in sleep.

XVI

O rare and holy, O taper lit for me
Before vast altars in the lonely dark,—
Without your gleam, dim were my soul to see
Where in star-spaces, imperial and stark
And sacrosanct, his ancient thronèd reign
God holds o'er stars and swallows as of yore;
Up through his Gothic vault I yearned in vain
And turned back baffled from him evermore.
In secular joys I must interpret heaven;
In ecstasies profane I must embrace
His glory,—seek in revels lightning-riven
All I shall ever witness of his face,—
And in wild flight, with passion winged and shod,
Circle and beat the citadel of God.

XVII

The entrails of a cat,—some rusty wood,—
Certain pegs, pins, in curious manner bent,—
These yield the spirit in its singing mood
The one supreme heaven-scaling instrument.
And I, who rate man's clay not overmuch,
Marvel not more when from the bow-swept strings
Celestial music soars, than when we touch
From mortal flesh strains of immortal things.
To worlds beyond the world of its resort
The viol uplifts its ecstasy or despair.—
O love, who knows what white Hyperian court
Welcomes our spirits, through the cloven air
Rising, beyond the instrument set free
On the wild wings of unloosed melody?

[79]

XVIII

Today, grown rich with what I late have won,
Across the dusk I reach my hand to you.
Cold as a leaf long pillowed on a stone
Your hand takes mine, like something strange and
    new.
So soon grown careless? . . . No, for in your eyes
A tenderness still lives, half-shy, half-bold . . .
Then sudden wisdom to my trouble cries:
I know you still my love, but not the old.
That which I loved and won now all is gone;
She was an hour, a moment, a swift mood,—
Vanished forever into deeps unknown,—
And a new creature rules your brain and blood.
Yesterday you were mine, beloved and fair:
Today I seek: another love is there.

XIX

There stretch between us wonder-woven bonds,
Fine as a thread but strong as braided steel,—
A link that to each changing need responds,
Nor binds the butterfly upon the wheel.
For the coarse bondage sanctioned of men's law
I would not, though I could, these gossamers
    change,—
Give time and circumstance that leave to draw
Closer the net till nearness must estrange!
And yet a longing restless in me burns
To lock what never might the lock endure:—
As a glad sailor, sea-impassioned, yearns
That what he loves for being unsure, were sure,—
That the fierce doubtful splendor of bright foam
Might somehow, fierce and doubtful, light him
    home.

[80]

XX

I see the days stretch out in wavering line
Toward that sure day when we shall lie in mould.
What fate, I wonder, sordid or divine,
Within their close-shut hands for us they hold?
We have walked with the winds in chasmy places,
And been as birds down sea-born tempests flung,—
Seen joy and wonder on each other's faces,
And learned that life is maddening still, and young.
Will the slow days cancel,—or reconcile,—
These with more sober meanings that they bring?
Shall we part bitter, or with humorous smile,
Or with heart-rent tragic remembering?—
Or sink in friendship, each a tired guest
Who finds the dreamless fireside slumber best?

XXI

Now jewelled, alight, you lead the midnight dances.
A thousand eyes, a hundred hearts are yours.
In the great hall, the splendor of your glances
With beauty's secret promise lights and lures.
They flock to you; you smile; they press around
  you
And crave your favors each with satyr smile.
Does your look lie, or do they truly sound you
With flatteries that your warming heart beguile?
See—the low lustful thinly maskèd faces!
They crowd about you, drinking in your bloom.
In fancy, each a taxi calls, and races
With you to his own Sybaritic room. . . .
I sit alone beneath my desk-lamp's glare,
Cursing the fate that made you mine, and fair.

XXII

What is he but a common gutter-cur,
A chattering mountebank, obese and base?
And yet perhaps your judgment may prefer
His grinning to my thin and furrowed face.
My rival! . . . How the word burns on my lips!—
Acknowledging equality, in that breath,
With him who is my equal but where slips
All form from life, and men are one in death.
He is with you now:—what words now from him
    fall?
What answering smile lights your alluring eyes?
Madness leers at me, as my thoughts recall
The love that late between us cried—and cries! . . .
Well, go! My mirth goes with you, who might be
A lamp of earth, a bright star from the sea.

XXIII

You are unworthy any man's desires.
I do suspect you of a thousand ills—
For little moths setting your little fires—
Haughty to high, servient to baser wills.
Rank! that the meanest prancer in your train
Can stir with languid love of lure your mood.
Is it your weak pleasure, or his weaker pain,
That gives sweet sustenance in this poor food?
You have seen visions of high luminous dawn
Coming to work a miracle in your heart:—
But now are veils across your watching drawn
Lest faith in viewless wonders plague your art. . . .
This light vain woman! What fit lash it were
Could I reveal the dream I held of her!

XXIV

You are not peace, you are not happiness;
I look not on you with content or trust;
Nor is there in you aught with power to bless
Or heal my spirit weary of life's dust.
No, you are that which, on a leaden day,
As endless clouds sluggish with rain pass by,
Leaps brilliant once across the sullen grey,
A vivid lightning-gleam in that dead sky.
And I, whose days of sun or cloud have grown
Changelessly furled in one grey monstrous pall,—
I thirst for fierce lights, triumphs, trumpets blown,
And you, most wild and passionate of all,—
You, the bright madness lightening the curse
Of reason's dull reign in the universe.

XXV

Today put by the tumult of our wars,
Where,—strangely sexless in that struggle,—vie
Our spirits, meeting mid the armored jars,
Eager to thwart, to torture, to defy.
Our souls were born for hostile dalliance.
And you, if onslaught of your malice fail,
Abase yourself, fain in my wounded glance
To read exultant that your stings prevail.
And yet, today, bar me not from my own.
Now I yield all surrender that is yours.
For we are weary; and, each one alone,
We front a world whose loneliness endures.
And there seem hours when o'er an evening deep
We might drift home. . . . I knew not you could
    weep!

XXVI

Fields far below us,—silence in the wood,—
Gold slanting rays down through green branches
    shed,—
You, clear against the hazy golden flood,—
And in your voice the summer as you said;
"I loved you once because a dream had come
Of what you might be,—and that was not you.
And once I hated, since my heart was numb
With pain to know my perfect hope untrue.
And once to make you other than you were
I would have mounted Calvary on bent knees.
But now,—dear lover whom such tempests stir,
I am forever done with all of these.
My love is yours:—be tender, fierce, or strange,—
You still are you, unchanged through every change."

XXVII

I have not brought you asphodel, or laid
Before you any pearl of happy prize.
We have been as great eagles, unafraid
Circling and grappling through tremendous skies.
But evening closes; and the tired wing
Slants downward in slow earth-approaching flight.
Over the regions of our voyaging
Are drawn the holy curtains of the night.
O weary one! O pitiful waif of space!
Here gleams the haven to our troubled quest;
This is the land sought of your yearning face;
This is the house dreamed of my lonely breast.
We who have known all agonies and all bliss,—
Can it then be we shall know happiness?

XXVIII

Now, O belovèd, in this pausing hour,
When peace, like a great river's twilight flow,
Isles us about from every alien power,
And all that hearts can know at last we know,—
Now let me speak words that within my breast
Have long, too long, dim to your passing view
Lain darkling, by a thousand storms oppressed,—
Now let me speak my holy love of you.
The topless peaks, the pure unclouded skies
That dwell remote within your spirit furled
I have not sung; and yet they filled my eyes,
Or how else had I sought you through the world?
My humors and my madness, fierce or cold,
I have told you all: my love I have not told.

XXIX

Through vales of Thrace, Peneus' stream is flowing
Past legend-peopled hillsides to the deep;
From Paestum's rose-hung plains soft winds are
    blowing;
The halls of Amber lie in haunted sleep;
The Cornish sea is silent with the summer
That once bore Iseult from the Irish shore;
And lovely lone Fiesole is dumber
Than when Lorenzo's garland-guests it wore.
This eve for us the emerald clearness glowing
Over the stream, where late was ruddy might,
Whispers a wonder, dumb to other knowing,—
Known but to you, the silence, and the night.
Our boat drifts breathless; the last light is dying;
Stars, dawn, shall find us here together lying.

[85]

XXX

Low suns and moons, long days and spacious nights,
With majesty move by us; and in state,
Like buskined actors treading tragic heights,
Enlarge the measure of our common fate.
Across the great gold-hazèd afternoon
Drifts deeper meaning than our thought can prove;
And happy dusks and happy dawns too soon
Beyond our sight in calm procession move.
Dear, hospitable, grows the murmuring earth;
As lords at home,—masters returned from wars,—
Rule we this realm whose summer-thronèd worth
Admits no craving for the distant stars.
Close suns and moons, wide nights and spacious
    days,—
The Gods once sojourned in these earthly ways!

XXXI

. . . I held no trust in this, that it should last!
Of no malignant fates stand I the sport!
If any memory plague me with the past,
I of most clear foreknowledge make retort.
What are the powers that at earth's center live
That such a dream as ours they should permit?
Why, Heaven itself would have no more to give
If Hell allow we should not wake from it!
Dreaming, I saw beyond the curtained dream,—
Half-conscious ever of the stubborn day
Waiting to smite our turrets, high a-gleam,
With armored siege of hurtling ray on ray.—
What would you have, dear lady?—who, for love,
Did ask the world that from its course it move?

[86]

XXXII

Yet no! . . . The thwartings of malignant chance
Shall set no bar to our impassioned trust!
I will assail these gates of circumstance
And break their iron hinges to the dust. . . .
Why are you pallid in the eye of the sun?
Do cold winds blow you from the midmost fire?
Or does the journey ere 'tis well begun
Speak with less eager lure to your desire? . . .
Your look corrodes the metal of my heart. . . .
Are we then tainted with a pallid cast
Of ghostly moonlight? All the foes that start
From ambush do not fright me as this last,
This sudden web of weakness round us grown. . . .
One gate we cannot storm. It is our own. . . .

XXXIII

Last night I kissed you with a brutal might
Whereof clanged echoes hunt me from my rest.
And bitter on my lips that fierce delight
Lingers, and bitter the pressure of your breast.
I am shaken, still, by the tumult of that hour
Before the dawn, when in some traitor-mood
You, upon whom love's beauty kept no power,
Lay vanquished by love's sensual habitude.
And ere the cock-crow you denied us thrice,
Being sure that all our daring dreams had lied.
Like an arc of fire then leaped my sacrifice,
My kiss of hate on the lips that had denied,—
A gift of the flesh, since the soul you dared not
      meet. . . .
And I longed that my kiss should strike you dead
      at my feet.

XXXIV

So you go back,—because they bid you come
And stand with them to prove the tales untrue,—
Until at last the whispers shall grow dumb,
And men forget the thing they guessed or knew.
And as the folly of an hour, at most,
Our love shall be remembered down the years—
A brightness dust-obscured, a vision lost,
Shall be the secret of our passionate tears.
To them,—I seem a rogue who half-succeeded,
And you, frail beauty almost led astray.
All the fierce splendor that our spirits needed
Already fades, a ghost of yesterday.
Well then, go back! To your dead gods be true.
What can you say to me, or I to you?

XXXV

Then go. I do not want you. It is over.
The flickerings of our dream have had their day.
Imagine now that he who was your lover
Has sunk in drink, or died, or moved away.
And all that flamed between us once is older
Than hopes that died before our lives began.
Summer is done for us; the dusks grow colder;
We are not gods, but futile woman and man.
With ineffectual will and dazzled eyes
We sought a faith beyond our power to make. . . .
The potter, as the dizzying swift wheel flies,
Must guard his spirit lest his fingers shake
And the vase lie in ruin. . . . It is over,—
Potter, and pot, and bad clay, and weak lover.

[88]

XXXVI

I have divested my dim spirit now
Of its great ornament, and bid go by,
Beyond the call of any prayer or vow,
The star so long the center of my sky.
Void,—grey and limitless,—now lies ahead—
Where my strange orbit, circling on alone,
Through regions of the living or the dead
May find wide gulfs that shall for light atone.—
Wide gulfs, bleak darkness, iron ecstasy
Amid my blind and frozen fellow-stars!—
Some flight of more than human history,
Some peace more terrible than all life's wars,
Some undiscovered depth of ancient night
But never you, never again the light.

XXXVII

Over profoundest deeps, light lacy foam
Plays where the sun-world frontiers meet the sea's.
And in the deeps, slow gulf-tides have their home,
Nor is the foam-crest utterant of these.
Sail the bright surface on a summer's day,
And you shall dream along each smiling crest,
Making the waves companions of your play,
Blind to the glooms within the ocean's breast.
But when grey weather muffles up the blue,
And thundering voices rise from hollow deeps,
And coldly drooping wraith-mist out of view
Inviolate the ancient mystery keeps,—
Then would you know the secret ocean-world,
Then dive!—a plummet through vast shadows
    hurled.

XXXVIII

What Beatrice was, so much you are
To me now wandering with an exile's eyes
In regions whence no road to paradise
Mounts, and the solace glimmers of no star.
There stretch between us gulfs of many a war;
The ancient hills to sunder us arise.
And yet I crave, from Fate that all denies,
You near in dream, who are in truth so far. . . .
*"Though all the powers that thwart your life and
     mine*
Thereto consent, yet can I never be
Your Beatrice. I can never shine
Pale, starry in your heaven; nay, unto me
One lot alone my stormy fates assign—
To leave you,—or to clasp you utterly!"

XXXIX

What if some lover in a far-off Spring,
Down the long passage of a hundred years,
Should breathe his longing through the words I
     sing—
And close the book, dazed by a woman's tears?
Does it mean aught to you that such might be? . . .
Ah! we far-seekers! . . . Solely thus were proved
From dream to deed the souls of you and me:—
Thus only were it real that we had loved.
Grey ghosts blown down the desolate moors of
     time!
Poor wanderers, lost to any hope of rest!
Joined by the measure of a faltering rhyme!
Sundered by deep division of the breast!—
Sundered by all wherein we both have part;
Joined by the far-world seeking of each heart.

XL

I needs must know that in the days to come
No child that from our Summer sprang shall be
To give our voices when the lips are dumb
That lingering breath of immortality.
Nay, all our longing compassed not such hope,
Nor did we, in our flame-shot passagings,
Push the horizon of our visions' scope
To regions of these far entangled things.
I knew not such desire.   But now I know.—
O perfect body!   O wild soul a-flower!
We, wholly kindled by life's whitest glow,
Turned barren from our life-commanding hour. . . .
Now while I dream, sweetness of that desire
Lies on my heart like veils of parching fire. . . .

XLI

This is a record of what has not been,
Is not, and never while time lasts can be.
It is a tale of lights down rain-gusts seen,—
Of midnight argent mad moon-archery.
Ah, life that vexes all men plagued us most!
And made us motes in winds that blew from far,—
Credulous of the whispers of a ghost,—
Fain of the light of some long-quenchèd star.
What were you that I loved you?   What was I
That I perturbed you?   Shapes of restless sleep!
A shadow from a cloud that hurried by,—
A ripple of great powers that stirred the deep.
And we, too supple for life's storms to break,
Writhed at a dream's touch, for a shadow's sake!

XLII

Across the shaken bastions of the year
March drives his windy chariot-wheels of cold.
Somewhere, they tell me, Spring is waiting near . . .
But all my heart is with things grey and old:—
Reliques of other Aprils, that are blown
Recklessly up and down the barren earth;
Mine the dull grasses by the Winter mown,
And the chill echoes of forgotten mirth.
Spring comes, but not for me. I know the sign
And feel it alien. I am of an age
That passes. All the blossoms that were mine
Lie trampled now beneath December's rage.
Ye children of the Spring, may life be sweet!
For me, the world crumbles beneath my feet.

XLIII

There are strange shadows fostered of the moon,
More numerous than the clear-cut shade of day. . . .
Go forth, when all the leaves whisper of June,
Into the dusk of swooping bats at play,—
Or go into that late November dusk
When hills take on the noble lines of death,
And on the air the faint astringent musk
Of rotting leaves pours vaguely troubling breath.—
Then shall you see shadows whereof the sun
Knows nothing,—aye, a thousand shadows there
Shall leap and flicker and stir and stay and run,
Like petrels of the changing foul or fair,—
Like ghosts of twilight, of the moon, of him
Whose homeland lies past each horizon's rim. . . .

XLIV

The clouds that steal across the sun of June
Are swift; and out of them the sun comes free.
The mists that drift beneath the flying moon
Reveal new brightness of her wizardry.
Not so the shadows that on the spirit fall,
Moving like torrents that wind the mountain-steep.
Down from the slopes they bear beyond recall
Earth and flowers; their pathway is graven deep.
They wear the iron rock; they change the hills;
The slopes are torn; the peaks fall; the vales flood
    wide.
And when the waters cease, and sound of rills
Remains, the battle's echo, down the mountain-side,
Passers-by shall marvel, in far-off days—
"Here lie forever the torrent's ancient ways!"

XLV

They brought me tidings; and I did not hear
More than a fragment of the words they said.
Their further speech died dull upon my ear;
For my rapt spirit otherwhere had fled—
Fled unto you in other times and places.
Old memories winged about me in glad flight.
I saw your lips of longing and delight,—
Your grave glad eyes beyond their chattering faces.
I saw a world where you have been to me
More than the sun, more than the wakening wind.
I saw a brightness that they could not see.
And yet I seemed as smitten deaf and blind.
I heard but fragments of the words they said.
Life wanes. The sunlight darkens. You are dead.

XLVI

Out of the dusk into whose gloom you went,
Answer me, tell me, why you chose to go?
Why did you seek that far-strewn firmament?
Was loneliness not keen enough below?
Did some old wrong affright you? Some new ill?
Did one more bloom that lured you turn to dust?
What spur could goad that lovely weary will,
What hopeless calm, what storm of shaken trust?
Across the giant waste of this unknown
Must I forever send my questionings?
Had you no word to leave me for my own
Before you went? Must my imaginings
Deem you forgot?—Or did your heart foretell
That time's whole later hush would speak farewell?

XLVII

Now from the living fountains of my thought
What stream of comfort, crystalline and mild,
Shall cool the wound the sudden stroke has wrought
And bid my heart in peace be reconciled?
My spirit whispers—"From this meteor flown,
Draw knowledge of the stars, now all is done.
Assign it station in some system known,
Part of the ordered brightness round the sun."
Good counsel!—reconcile, transmute, remould
To earth's conglomerate mass this unconfined
Pilgrim of sky,—or label it, grown cold,
To edify a chaos-fearing mind? . . .
Love, love, I keep memorial of you! Nay!—
Unsolved, bright, lonely, till my Judgment Day!

An April Elegy

I

"Over my organ-keys in the twilight
If I but let my wandering fingers
Stray at their will, would they not, out of muted
Notes and broken sequences and diminished
Chords, evoke a ghostly echo of you?—
Chanting slowly in the ambiguous darkness
More than a resurrection of our old choral,—
Freeing at last the shadowy fugue beyond you
That I divined and loved, but never knew?

"Sidonian lute!
Still tremulous with music. . . .
Sidonian lute!
Whose breasts were lilies. . . .

"Over these keys, growing dim in the twilight,
Slowly, confusedly, wander my fingers,
Impotent now to build, from the muted
Notes and broken sequences and diminished
Chords, an echo of you.
Chanting solemnly now in the deepening darkness
Rises the host of implacable memories.
Into the darkness dies the wandering music,
And I remember the poignant you alone."

[95]

II

One April night, when the slow drip of rain
Like a remote accompaniment
Upon her window-pane
Played ghostly threnodies,
And they were very close, while in the trees
Outside the window the cold arc-lights set
A thousand stars
On branches gleaming wet,
While the belovèd mystery of the dark
Swept like a curtain over the soiled park,—
Then, as her head
Upon his shoulder rested
Like a bird nested,—
But on that night indifferently,—then he said:
"If you should die,
You who have made me happy and tortured me
With your inscrutable soul's perversity,
Then I
Would mark your memory with such wreath of
    song
As to no other woman might belong
Through all of history."
And in the rapt indifference of her face,—
For at that hour her love was far away,—
A little mocking tenderness found place;
He heard her say:

"Poor player! I would die,—save that the test
Would rob you of more rest
Than even my perversity of now.
Dear dreamer! painfully that vow

Would haunt your sleep forever.
No, for your sake I will forbear to sever
The thread of life.   And though I cannot smile
With quite the madness that I once could use,
It seems that I must choose
To save you from your oath, and live a little
    while. . . ."

   The rain came down
Quietly, steadily, over the town.
They sat, silent; he dreaming of the lays
Which in fantastical coronal of praise
He would have woven for her were she dead.
And then she fell asleep, her light smooth head
Upon his shoulder. . . .
Tonight the rain
Beats on his window-pane—
The fierce rain of a Spring but one year older. . . .

III

   "Now Paris, grey with April, as though
       November
Instead of Spring were here,
Hushes its happy voices; to my ear
Come only echoes; and as I remember,
In sudden gleams there rises, swirls, and passes
Image on image of our tarnished fate.
Belovèd ghost,—under your rain-swept grasses,
Do you too love them, now it is too late?

   "Sidonian lute!
Sidonian lute!
Into the darkness dies the wandering music,
And I remember the poignant you alone. . . ."

IV

Twice only in his life and hers they met:
One meager day, two fleeting nights;
Flaming with meteor-lights
Or where the grey rains set
Their curtains to sway and fret;
Once in the sun and moon,
Once in the dusk and rain;
Passionate once with June
Singing a maddening tune,
And once again
Shadowed and hushed and strange with ghosts of
      voiceless pain. . . .

V

"Music! Music!
I cannot wake you.
For the Sidonian lute
Has gone into the darkness;
And now my fingers on the lifeless organ
Fail; and I turn to memories alone."

VI

The dreary drizzle of white rain at last
Broke, that June morning, into crystal air.
Still round him clung from the three days now past
A meaningless monotony of despair.
For three days he had paced his paneled room
And watched a beaten miry universe;
While ever closer to him drew the gloom
His desultory music could not pierce.

[98]

Bedraggled passers, dripping beasts and carts,
Infrequently and darkly plodded by
Like desperate external counterparts
Projected from his spirit's misery.
The real world and the world of his own thought
Had been a waste, blank and of bitter fate;
And every chain of woven chords he wrought
Had jangled off to chaos, desolate.

Now he looked forth, and saw the bays were
white
With the contagion of the wind's delight,
And up the red cliffs of the coast
The high foamed waves were tossed.
Full of a cold and self-corrosive mirth
He wandered forth
Out of his lonely house; and straying down
Passed through the scattered town
Whose uncouth streets and fishy smells again
Struck discords in his brain.

Then as his brooding way
Led round the headlands of a rocky bay,
He saw ahead a little white-winged boat
Aimlessly drifting,
Just off the shore afloat
Dipping and lifting,—
In it an unknown girl who toward the land
Stood gazing.   And he watched her moveless stand
And measure him with curious scrutiny.
Then suddenly, with a gesture toward the sea,
She broke the silence—"Will you come and sail with
me?"

Her eyes were stranger than her words;
Like the swift flight of young adventurous birds
They sought the far horizon, and then turned
Again to him with laughing look that burned
Like June alight.
She stood poised, slender, dressed in flashing white,
Close to the sail, deep blue of sky around.
And for a moment they gazed without a sound;
Till, smiling to see him dumb,
She shot the boat to the rock-edge of the land,
Held out her hand,
And said—"Come!"

Why should she mock him? . . . Then he knew
Not mocking, but a crazy whim,
Spoke in her words.   And as the blue
Of sea and sky swept over him,
A flash of her preposterous mood
Dispelled the lethargy of his brain.
The summer wakened in his blood;
He stumbled into life again.

"Come?   Yes!" he said, "although I fear and
    think
You are a mermaid, to some fishy brink
Plotting to draw me down!"
She laughed—"No, no!   Behold, I have two feet!
I am indubitably a mortal and complete.
I will not let you drown!"

He came; she loosed the fluttering sail,
And out across the bay they soared.
No speech,—for what could that avail
Here where the wind and sea were lord?

[100]

He marveled at her laughing glance,
Her careless and imperious way;
And thought—"For once, a kindly chance
Brings me a madcap holiday!"—
And to the whimsy of her jest
Became a full conspirator.
The boy within him, long repressed,
Awoke to match the girl in her.
Their eyes that turned from sky and wave
Met sometimes with a comrade-smile,
And sometimes with a wonder, grave
Of speculation. And the while
They rushed through waters lifting strong
Bright spires of foam into the sun;
Across their cheeks the wind's keen song
Dashed till they felt its trumpets run
Along their veins, an heroic shout;
And to each other smiled again
As the boat's prow dipped in and out
Of crested breakers down the plain.

  Her blowing hair was like dark mist
Hiding sometimes her eyes and brow
And delicate curve of cheek; her wrist
And arm moved white, holding the bow
With tiller hard into the gale.
The rondure of her throat was bare,
And half her shoulder, cloudy-pale,
Behind its covering glimmered there.
Her eyes were touched with steady light.
As league on league swept rushing by,
Amid the friendly fierce sea-might
Each glance became a glad reply

Of spirits from the tangled days
Released to meet in boundless space.
He watched her swift and eager ways
And changing lights across her face;
And caught her fire,—the flush of one
Fled from the cities to beguile
A tired heart, where wind and sun
Could charm her for a little while
With simpler touch of primal things
And blot away the echoing feet
And intricate importunings
Of life too crowded and too fleet.

Remote seemed all the wonted faces—
They were adventurers of the wind.
They swept into vast unknown spaces—
How far the day-world lay behind!
The tumult of the waves began
To drown them in mad minstrelsy.
He seemed no more a brooding man
But a sure Triton of the sea;
And she behind her stormy hair
A water-wraith, a lightning-child,
A creature of the driven air
To earthly living half-beguiled.
Onward they sped, into the wide
Circle of restless seas and skies.
He drew more close, and at her side
Felt the blown spray whip in his eyes.
Were they above the waves, or under?
What matter, so they both could go?
She turned and looked at him, with wonder
Lighted, like golden foam aglow.

Her eyes had drunk the sunlight wholly;
There seemed no real world to forget;
And their hands touched and closed—and slowly
Their hesitant perturbed lips met.

Then were Titanic powers astir
Under the skies.
He clung to her
And she to him; their hands and eyes
Were locked in spell
As if each would some dawning miracle
Discover or foretell,
As the whole force
Of tumult gathered in its whitening course
Earth, sun, and sea.
He crushed her recklessly—
Her tremulous lips
Whirled his lost brain into a blind eclipse—
And when he saw again, it was to behold
The loose white fold
Of her gown slip from off her bright
Shoulder, and the gold might
Of the sun showered it with triumphant light.

And then
His head sank down against her naked breast—
With desperate arms he pressed
Her slender quivering body, drawn again
Closer to him, and thunderously knew
The winds that shook her being through and
    through,
And knew her cry for him, as thus maddeningly
    they strove
In storm of love.

. . . Suddenly, as one
Awakening from a dream,
She shivered, and turned . . .
The madness was gone;
The flame that burned
A moment since, now on the stream
Of some fresh current of her soul glided into the
    void away.
Dimly he heard her say
With tortured smile—
"Not that, not that! Oh let us only be happy a
    little while!"

And he released her; and without a word
Onward they sped
Toward where the westering sun its cataract poured
On waves ahead;
Baffled and chilled and full of fear
Whither the way might tend,
But knowing well that this dumb struggle here
Was not the end.

VII

"Oh troubled music drifting down the twilight
With flutes and cymbals of some old confusion,
Lighting the darkness, striking across the darkness
With flame of voices and tumultuous breath!" . . .

VIII

That night the sun went down at last
When evening in a blaze of gold
Sank behind amethystine veils.
Drifting along the bays they passed

With faint airs breathing and manifold
Whispers amid their tranquil sails.
And high above the cliffs, the moon
Her naked silver majesty
Above this hush of glowing June
Unveiled to haunt the sleeping sea.
And they were tranquil,—even they
Who late in such a storm had tossed
Now musingly in dusk of grey
Sailed up the long line of the coast.

Now he had come to know her face
And see the delicate moulding there
Where intricate thoughts had carved their trace
Of fineness more than merely fair—
The scarcely hollowed cheek, the eyes
Of never-resting eagerness,
The wide white brow,—seemed deeply wise
Behind their glow of youthful dress.
Thoroughly wise, that face, and versed
In what world, flesh, and devil meant;
And yet, for all it had rehearsed,
Irrevocably innocent.—
A child's face, almost,—one who played
With dangerous toys for her delight
And tossed sharp daggers unafraid
Yet never stabbed her bosom quite.—
The groves of Sidon seemed to stir
Beyond the shadows of her hair.
An ancient sadness circled her
With light that fallen queens might wear.
Her cool and pallid beauty bore
No likeness to the summer's blooms;

It breathed of myrrh from some far shore,
Of secret winds, of rock-cut tombs.——
A face that from the lighted crowd
Might haunt a lonely passer's thought
And whisper where the streets are loud
Forgotten musics he had sought.

And yet amid the silences
Came doubts of ominous intent.
He felt astray in mysteries,
Unsure what this adventure meant.
Beyond her sweetness, siren-eyed,
Beyond her unrevealing smile,
What strange chimera shapes might hide
Of proved debasement, daring guile,
As of some mere adventuress,
Some Babylonian, shrewd to spice
A fundamental wantonness
With moonlight of mock paradise?

Then as her voice across the dark
Came, slender, modulated, cool,
He knew his fancies for the stark
Perversions of a skeptic fool.
He knew that whatsoever lord
Of flame or chaos ruled in her
Was brother to the flashing sword
Of the high rebel, Lucifer.

There was a tenderness in the night;
She seemed no stranger to his eyes.
He talked unguarded with delight
And caught the throb of her replies.
He followed where her laughter led

Up airy flights of some conceit,
And all the low-toned words she said
Chimed individual and sweet
Within his mind.   Of dreams and men,
Cities and songs, that they had loved
They gravely argued, laughed again,
Echoed and answered and approved.
He long had moved in middle air,
Not quite a denizen of earth,
Weaving his wandering music there
Where meteors come to flashing birth;
And now this secret region, dumb
And icy to the general heart,
He saw with wonder, was her home . . .
Wherein her spirit moved apart
Upon some ever-baffled quest
Of beauty, happiness, or all
That can allure the mortal guest
To leave the mortal festival.
And he, who late had solely known
The call of her enraptured blood,
Now felt her spirit and his own
Freed in a luminous quietude
Wherein even her loveliness
Seemed but the secret minister
Of the live soul intense to press
Out through each line and hue of her.

   In the wide silver glow
Over their empty ocean shed
They drifted into silence.   Then he said—
"We, strangers, know
Each other strangely well tonight.

But this is a faery-land afar.—
In regions of the common light
I wonder who you really are?"

She smiled a little.—"You I know quite well,
And your high grey monastic house
Looking down on the coast.
And how each summer you dwell
There like a hermit, with forbidding brows
And eyes in dreaming lost!
And that from out the organ's sleeping keys
You summon visions and spells and mysteries.
But I,—the words would tell
You nothing; for of late
I have thrown aside my old self and old name
And the old world that I had come to hate.
No, this is faery-land; you must not claim
To know my earthly fate."
And he asked nothing further, being content
To dwell a while in her enchanted maze
By delicate sweetness lighted through and through.
He knew not whence she came nor where she went;
And who she was, even in the later days
He never fully knew.

Oh night of wonder! Down the wide
Slow-heaving flood they slowly passed.
She seemed a dream-shape; at her side
He only hoped the dream might last.
Each shadowy headland came to loom
Like a great monster, till the tide
Swept them around it, and the gloom
Turned silver on the farther side.
Hour after hour they slipped along,

Silent or speaking as they willed.
The night seemed gloriously long
And with a dream's long wonders filled.

At last the reddening moon hung low
Over the water; and its glow
Was a wide track of broken light,
A pathway for them down the night—
Till it sank; and on the deep
An impenetrable veil of sleep
Seemed spread above the quiet foam,
Save where, in the gigantic dome
Of dark, the stars' slow pageantry
Wheeled in solemn glory by.

Then for long they never spoke.—
Until, far eastward, broke
A faint light through the dark,
And the swift, stark,
Bewildering dawn began to come
Mysteriously cold across the foam
From the remote horizon. They leaned out
From the little boat
And felt the coolness of the stirring air,
Speculatively marking where
The sun at last would lift
Its rim. They seemed adrift
As in the first dawn seen by the first man,
It was all so vast, so measureless, so new.
She shivered, and drew
A little closer to him; and then his frame began
To tremble also with some inward power
Awakening slowly.
She turned and looked at him; the unearthly hour,

The silence, the lone world, suddenly seized them
    wholly,—
And with a cry, throwing aside the weight
Of the confused night's obscure history
And all the wisdom of the day now past,
Upon their lips came the salt sting of fate;
And the irresistible flood of bursting light
Swept them with sacred might
Out to the dusky passion-shaken sea
Of each other's arms, each other's breasts at
    last. . . .

  When the sun came
With clear flame,
She, dumb but smiling, turned toward shore;
And where, the day before,
She had found him, steered along the edge
Of the rocky ledge.
He kissed her lips and shoulder, and stepped forth
To the real earth.
Then out unswervingly through the blue heart of
    the bay
She sailed away.

IX

"Over my organ-keys in the twilight
Slowly, aimlessly, wander my fingers,
Impotent now to build, from the muted
Notes and broken sequences and diminished
Chords, an echo of you.
Chanting slowly now in the deepening darkness
Rises the host of implacable memories.
Into the darkness dies the wandering music,
And I remember the poignant you alone."

X

He sought his house, and flung himself upon the
    bed
And slept.
Within that darkened room, all day, around his
    head
Wild shadows kept
A ceaseless troubled watch; vague dreams
Flickered and died; he drifted
Down endless winding streams
Beside her, silent; and then was lifted
Suddenly up into tempestuous air
Where he and she were hurled
Headlong across the spaces of the world
In terror and confusion of all thought.
And then she was gone; and he in torture sought
Her vanished form down deserts, and down streets
Of multitudinous cities clanging loud,
And seemed to find and lose her in the crowd
And come on her once more where traffic meets
Cross-streaming traffic. There one look of hers
Would light his heart,—then she was gone again,
Swept by the eddy of trampling hosts apart
From the starved hope of his despairing brain.

When he awoke
Out of this troubled drowse, more trance than sleep,
An ashy yellow light of sunset broke
Across the sky; and under it the steep
Huge slopes of leaden clouds along the west
Were stretched, with dull fire smouldering in their
    breast.

Then as the dusk fell over the still sea
And a vast emptiness hushed the twilight space,
He walked the heights, a slave to memory,
Seeking the contours of her vanished face.
This should have been a light adventure, cast
Into the void when parting words were said:
Why did the troubling echo of beauty last?
Why was he dreaming, now the hour was fled?
On every breeze he almost caught the tone
Of her low voice; and every curve of bough
Recalled a sense of beauty that was gone.
She seemed so far, and he more lonely now.
Along the coolness of the evening air
Stole the sweet coolness of her delicate cheek;
And all the perfume of her showering hair
Drifted from darkness on him. He grew weak
And lonely as a child to have her stroke
His hair with some small pitying caress.
His memory now seemed powerless to evoke
One clear-cut aspect of her loveliness.
Where was she now? he wondered. Did she brood
Now in some waste of agony and shame,
Finding beyond the night's delirious mood
Only regretful ashes of spent flame?
Humiliation and distrust and hate,—
Perhaps these thoughts companioned her tonight . . .
Could he but see her!—speak his sense of fate
That once in all the years had wrought aright!
Could he but kiss her quiet forehead,—bring
His thanks for loveliness that saves and frees,—
The night should drift above them on hushed wing
And loosened tears flow in the silences.

[112]

Then down the night drifted a jangling sound
Of laughter as his heart revived its fears.
What if he were the dupe of some profound
And facile guile,—and all his starting tears
Were wasted at the feet of one who now
Whispered this tale to some fresh worshiper
Down the smooth floors where suave adorers bow,
And ready mirth flamed up to circle her?
Clumsily, doubtless, he had played his part,
Unversed in gallantry, too deeply stirred.
He seemed to hear her mock his dreaming heart
And ape his smile and quote his fatuous word. . . .

And then he cursed his skeptic heart, intent
To ruin every flower with blight.
That haunting music was no dream that went
With silver footsteps down the night!
Some luminous recollection came to kill
The specters of his doubt and his distress;
And well he knew, tonight she was grave and still
Under the shadow of lost loveliness.

Like a white bird gone over the white wave
She gleamed before his thought that followed her.
Delicate, subtle, lonely-hearted, brave,
She had come to him, a young deliverer,
A goddess from the foam.   Now down her track
His heart pursued with longing and despair;
And knew, not all his passion could bring back
The murmur of her voice, or her dim hair.

His lips were quivering with her cool soft lips.
His hand stretched out to touch her carven breast.
Below him in the harbor sleeping ships

[113]

Filled him with hatred of their dreamless rest. . . .
Then to escape the alien majesty
Of the white planets wheeling slowly by,
He turned and entered to his paneled room
Where few lights hazed the gloom.—

And over his organ-keys all night
His fingers strayed, searching through shifting
    mazes
For her and for the echoes of her delight;
Tracking her up the stair of singing keys,
Through vaults and naves of sound,
And deep into sepulchral crypts profound,
And into sudden flights through sunlit air,
And through pale hazes
Of moonlight, dreaming above waters wide
Where music drifted like an ancient tide
Over a sea-washed city, or where on high
A rock-perched swan beneath moon-flooded sky
Poured out its heart in desperate melody.

XI

"Into the darkness dies the wandering music—
Into the darkness again dies the wandering music,
Echoing you, echoing you alone."

XII

At last
After long weeks that kept him still astir
With memories of voices faintly heard,
At last
There came a written word
From her.

. . . "And all day long,
And all the after night,
You were with me like the cadence of a song
I had half-forgotten. And I tried to write,
But there were people around me, every hour;
And on the following day there were more and
    more.
And when at length I was alone, my power
Of speech had left me; I was tired, and bore
The weight of silence,—as I have done before.

"Tonight I sail—tonight upon the sea
I shall surely think of a thousand things unsaid
To tell you.   Oh, send your love after me!
I do not know what lies ahead . . .
The ocean, yes, and Havre,—and then at last
My dear Paris, where all my youth was passed
In exile. Now, returning, it seems home.
I do not go to paint.— Do you know Vendôme,
And Blas, and Browne, and Wallace, and Hélène
    Coudray?—
I do not go to work,—only to play
With them and all the others. Yes, I go . . .
Good-bye, oh lover dearer than I could know!

"Our day and night was flawless—that was why
I said good-bye
So suddenly—
Fearing some act or word
Might rise to break its beautiful accord.
Yes, I was passionately afraid
That if you stayed
With me for nights and days we would tarnish even

That unique heaven
In which for one glad hour our feet had strayed.
And yet,—when you were gone
I wept, for I seemed very much alone.

"Now everything around me.
Is tangled, doubtful, beautiless, insecure.
My dear, you found me
In a strange hour, too exquisite to endure.
And now—my thoughts are dizzy for want of sleep,
And far too many people round me keep
Moving and moving restlessly—
And yet I would have it so, poor foolish I!

"Good-night! Tonight the moon's adrift
Upon the little winds that blow
Over a sea without a stain.
Here is my love for you:—poor gift!
Perhaps,—who knows?—I do not know,—
I will not see you again."

Dull pain of loss throbbed in him; now she seemed
Herself a moon vanishing down the west—
Not the great flaming light he late had dreamed,
But a lonely slender wraith, stealing to rest.
Gone!—and no more of what had been so much . . .
Why must the splendor pass so swiftly by?
Her words, like lingering of a farewell touch,
Drew out his heart to follow miserably.

Days passed . . .
He turned at last
Into the ordered life he long had known.
Dreams came
[116]

And April flame
Awoke, as when a smouldering coal is blown,
With memories of her.   Yet he somehow moved
With steady step along the common earth,
Unwilling that a chance wind he had loved
Should shake the oak-trees of more ancient worth.
And scarcely would he then unto himself confess
How perfumes, textures, curves of loveliness
Swept him sometimes,—till he cried out to her,
Belovèd comforter.

   At length,—not weeks, but months,—one penciled
     note
Came to him from her.   Thus she wrote—

   "Oh I am happy today, my dear!
This is a miracle-day!
If you were here and I were here
We'd quickly run away—
Out to the Bois, to a charming inn
That you, too, surely know,
Deep in the wood, where the city's din
Never dares to go.
And there we would sit us down to dine
Like Babes in love in the Wood,
And be, with our goblets of yellow wine,
Too happy to be good!

   "Ah well!
This is no age to ask a miracle! . . .

   "I have not written a letter for so long?
My dear, it would have been a mournful song
I should have piped!   You see, I have been trying
To become happy—and I started wrong;

At least it all ended in only crying . . .
Also I have been tired, horribly tired. —And yet
Have I? Today I am so glad, surely I can for-
    get. . . .

    "Oh such a day! Adorable! The sun and the
    cool air
Over the city spread a dream: at Armenonville,
    where
The Bois is charming, it must be quite maddeningly
    fair.

    "I wish that you were here to play—with me:
    you play so well.
And if you were here would you play? Or will you
    never tell?
I do assure you that tonight I am most playable!

    "Stupid of you!—I want to talk,—and you are
    far away!
Perhaps next Spring you will come to me, some other
    happy day?
But we shall be other people then . . . Life mocks
    us . . . Who can say?"

    His pulse leaped at the laughter in her words;
Joy swept his memory back to the perfect hour
Of their sea-love; her charm in echoing chords
Of sweetness thrilled him with prophetic power.
How he had needed her! Now, when the sun
Revived the happy music in her blood,
She turned to him, by touch of joy made one,
Sure that his heart would answer to her mood!

    And then
After a week she wrote again—

    [118]

"At last!—the quiet hour I have desired!—
And yet I am disconsolate, being alone.
I am so tired!
But now that they are gone—
The noisy company—and dawn is near
I am a-quiver with the fear
Of loneliness; my heart is like a stone.

"I am alone, and lonely.
That seldom happens now.
If you were here, would you bid me take a vow
Of rigorous seclusion? Oh if only
I could regain, in some inspired mood,
Courage for solitude!

"Tonight as through the gardens
Of the Luxembourg we trod
I knew I did not like my hat
And that there is no God.

"Don't hate me, oh my wisest, best!
Tonight be kind to me!
By all the world's futility
Tonight I am oppressed,—
And I,—I am the Supreme Futility.

"Have you seen how ridiculous
Up in their queer vague sky
The stars look from the city streets?
I saw them tonight. . . . Good-bye!"

Her shadowy pain fell on him. Was it all,—
Life's multiplex adventure and longing quest,—
But the procession of vain carnival

[119]

With no calm hour wherein the soul might rest?
And when at last concluding night should fall,
Was not perhaps the holy silence best? . . .

He moved in a troubled dreaming
As the months thereafter passed.
Wild notes from the void came streaming
To wreck each pattern he cast.
Till at length into the grey
Dusk of a winter's day
A letter came to fill
The twilight, and lead him away.—

"Everything is so different with me now!
I am too happy and too drowsed to write.
I am alone,—in bed;—the candle-light
Flickers beside me.   I cannot tell you how
Tranquilly, beautifully the world's a-shine
In spite of wind and beating gusts of rain
That sweep tormentedly against the pane
Of these dear rooms, these dear, dear rooms of
      mine!

"For these rooms are my liberty; they are wholly
Sacred and secret to my soul and me.
I have fled to them from the melancholy
Whirl of the sick world's phantom gaiety.
Too long I have been like a leaf of Fall
With mournful haste from revel to revel whirled.
But now I am the happiest heart of all!
I have regained my freedom from the world!

"How much I wish that you could see my rooms!
They are high in an old house, with lofty walls

And mullioned windows. There are gentle glooms
Across them when the evening sunlight falls
Golden out of the west most tenderly.
And the great city stretching far below
Grows but a distant doubtful dream to me
Into whose mazes I shall never go.

"Winter is passing by me; soon the Spring
Will make these skies a sapphire bubble clear. . . .
I wonder if its new-born life will bring
You by some miracle to see me here?
You must, you must! I will put on my best,
And be your guide through each minute, divine
Cranny and corner of this tower of rest,
These wonderful belovèd rooms of mine.

"Tonight I have so much to say
To you, you only; so much more
Than ever on any other day
To any mortal soul before.
But you are far from me. . . . I fear
My pen is impotent and dumb . . .
So much to say—and you not here!
Oh! will it last until you come?" . . .

XIII

"Under my touch the old impetuous music
Revives and cries a moment in the darkness,
Broken and wandering, with sudden echoes
That circle forth and seek for you alone."

XIV

That night out of his loneliness there grew
With slow deep strength a sense within his heart
That he must see her at whatever cost.

All other life seemed pale; at length he knew
Its tangled wastes unmeaning, here apart
From her he had so swiftly found and lost.

Restless, unhappy, daring, unconfined,
He felt her well to be.
An obscure warning flashed across his mind
That before,—yes, and after,—she
Had turned to other lovers. What were these
For him to hold as stain?
He loved her!—loved her subtle flashing brain
And her body's ecstasies.

Truly he judged her reckless, wild,
Unstable as a faery-child,—
Fatal and fickle and possessed
By demons that could never rest
In any love that he could give. . . .
And yet—how sweet it were to live
A while in her exotic spell
Of rapture!—while the miracle
Of love enthralled them,—while delight
Of her wild body lit the night
And her wild flashing spirit shone
Magical—till the hour was gone.
They with clear eyes and hearts awake
Might in their hour of April take
A day,—a month,—a year,—and bless
The gods for so much happiness.
For surely was that spirit wise
That hid behind her laughing eyes;—
Surely that spirit well did know
How the great miracles come and go,

And how the soul to death addressed
Must hail and speed the uncertain guest!
Perhaps she, too, was eager to cast
All shames away, and his at last
Become with him a soulless free
Mad nymph and faun in Arcady,—
Reckless, unmemoried, and gay
For this their pagan holiday.
Beautiful pagan that she was!
He saw her slender whiteness pass
Down valleys in wild laughing race
While he pursued, and the glad chase
Narrowed and closed, and panting fast
He clasped her in some dell at last.
Oh beauty, beauty called to him
Out of her maze, unsolved and dim
Of good and evil; and her name
Across his darkness shot its flame.

And then he grew to picture her
With him above the city's stir
In her high rooms, at twilight hour
Looking down as from a tower
On mortal life,—they two alone
Into one hour's completeness grown;
Touched with the sense of fleeting days,—
Life's sweetness, life's dear lingered ways,
Where for a moment, hand in hand,
Across the singing summer land
Of youth, two hearts may seek and hold
The rainbow's far incredible gold
And bid the daylight-world go by,
Content with their sole ecstasy.

He saw them wandering through the loud
Bright laughter of the midnight crowd
At other hours, delighting then
To feel the mysterious stream of men
Swirling around them, now a part
Of the great city's infinite heart.
And other days,—they drifting far
Down the small waterways of the Loire
Or Indre, where men are less than dreams
Upon the narrow willowed streams.
Perhaps they would grow simple there
Amid a world so mild and fair,—
Forget the intricate sodden maze
Of city nights and city days,
And blunder into peace, and be
Forgotten in felicity!

A dream! A dream! . . . Yet in a world
Whose verities in mists are furled,—
Where nothing is secure or plain
Save the realities of pain,
It seemed no madness. And the might
Of this gold vision came to smite
Its image on his brain; he felt
All fancied barriers break and melt.
And on a midnight when, alone,
His grey walls chilled him to the bone
With vague sepulchral prophecies,
And far away the wind-swept seas
Howled on their rocks, he suddenly stood
Transformed, and in adventurous mood
Knew her the meteor of his night,
Knew her his April of delight,

His flute of Spring, his golden west,
His sea-born and belovèd breast.

And in that night with terrible powers astir
He wrote to her.—

"I am coming now,
For I cannot be longer without you.
I am coming now,
And this is what my heart cries to you.—

"Sidonian lute!
Your breasts are lilies
Cooled by the dawn—
Your brain is lit
With summer lightnings—
Your thighs are sleeping music . . .
Sidonian lute!—
Pale lute awaiting
The musician's hand!—
Oh give me peace
From insupportable echoes. . . .

"Tonight—
This night before the summer—
Through which great winds
From remote storms
Rush secretly,—
On this night
I am drowned in your fragrance—
Devastated by you—
Mad with your memory. . . .

"Be merciful!
I kiss the ground before you,

I hold you in my arms
As a slave holds a pearl.
I am not I—
I am your shadow
That tracks you endlessly
Through star-swept spaces.
You—
Whose brain is lightning—
Whose breasts are lilies . . .
Sidonian lute!
Sidonian lute!
Whose breasts are lilies
Under the moon."

XV

"Over my organ-keys in the darkness
Slowly, aimlessly, wander my fingers,—
Slowly, aimlessly, silently, wander my fingers;
And I remember the poignant you alone."

XVI

At the dim head of the long winding stair
She waited, doubtful; the one gas-light's flare
Left the dusk round her shadowy and astir,
But outlined her
Sharply above him.   As that flame
Touched into life her unforgotten face,
He paused, and could not speak her name.
And she from her high place
Looked down, and knew him,—silent a moment's
    space,—
And then swiftly she cried—
"Why did you ring? Come, wanderer, inside,
    [126]

And see my wonderful rooms!—wonderful they
 were to be,
But some inertia has laid hold of me
And I have never done the things I planned.
Here a Thibetan altar was to stand,
And here my giant divan, one foot high,
Broad as the sky,
And covered with stripes of yellow and grey, indeed
 most marvelously!
But you are here, and nothing yet is done . . .
Turn, let me look at you, far-wandering one!"

 They sat upon a bare couch in that room
Vast and high-ceilinged, where the tender gloom
Of night was broken only by soft glows
From candle-shades of yellow touched with rose—
Sat and talked swiftly lest some strangeness come
Out of a pause of silence and make them dumb. . . .
With hungry eyes, he watched the quick moods
 chase
Each other across the sweet curve of her face,
And watched her turn and lift her eyes and smile
And speak and listen and look at him the while
With a bright friendly eagerness that was
Between them like a wall of shining glass.
There she sat,—beautiful, tender, within his
 grasp,—
And yet, for all his strength, he could not clasp
Her to him. An unsolved remoteness hung
In veils around her; and her eyes, that clung
To him, seemed searching for some difficult art
To thread the maze of his and her own heart.

They took each other's hands.—
"Yes, you are you," she said;
"And yet one understands
How for a moment strangeness will be shed
Between us as we speak; and only slowly
Shall we regain sense of each other wholly."
As they talked on
At first some part of her seemed changed or gone;
But then her voice would poise on a certain tone
With the old sweetness,
So that he knew she had not grown
Into another; yet some obscure completeness
Quite unremembered hung around her;
And a year's power had carved her delicate face
More intricately than when he first had found
    her,—
Shadowing forth out of their secret place
The gods and demons in her spirit furled
That made her *her*, unmatched in all the world.

"How long, how long it has been,"
She said; and to her questionings, then he told
Of the wide year and what had passed between,—
What labors he had ended, what manifold
New tasks he had begun; and how it seemed
That now at last the fame which he had dreamed
Some day should come to him began to shed
Its grateful warmth around his head
That had so long, lone and unhonored, bent
Over his organ-keys. Her delicate listening lent
To the dull tale a glamor,—made it glow
With more fulfillment than he had dared to know;
And all the long endeavor now seemed sweet
As he laid down the story at her feet.

"And you?" he asked.   But she
Only smiled at him softly, silently—
Then said—"I have written you letters! . . . No
    more, just now, of me."
   And then she took
From the low stool beside her a thin book
Saying—"Rest: you are tired"; and he lay
Upon the divan where she sat, her stray
Hand in his hand; his head was on her knees,
And thus he half embraced her; but wide seas
Lay unexplored between them.   As she read
Her hand crept to his head
And idly touched his hair
With as much quietude as the wandering air
Might so have used.   The delicate candle-light
Drew round them a small circle, with the night
Empty, tremendous, thunderously astir
Beyond the small oasis where they were,—
Beyond the little isle of glow where he and she
Lay side by side, sundered immeasurably.
   And very far away
Seemed that tempestuous day
When they had met.   Not at the place where last
They had parted could their spirits now embark,
But from a dark
And unknown spot.
They had come by separate paths to a new land:
Now they must stand
Doubtful in alien regions, and discover
What world this was,—whether of friend or lover
Or utter stranger.   And his hopes' bright wings
Sank baffled, beaten, lost amid this mist of shadow-
    ings.

XVII

"The music is silent now
In alien darkness.
And the Sidonian lute
Is silent in my soul.
Insupportable echoes
Drift from the alien darkness,
Crying of you,
Crying of you alone."

XVIII

At last she too
Desperately knew
That the words of her reading brought
Neither to him nor her meaning or thought
Or the inevitable painful speech they sought.
And throwing aside the volume she bent down
And, with a little frown
Lit by a smile, said to him tenderly—
"It is not what you thought that it would be?"

Pressing his shoulder closer to her side,
Striving to dull the loneliness of the hour,
He said—"Dear one, you know I cannot hide
From you that I have been a puppet in the power
Of an unearthly dream so long,—
Have been so long haunted, in toil or rest,
By memories of your sweetness, and clear song
Born of your lips, born of your maddening breast,—
That I am dizzied. Yet I understand
That there is nothing for you now to say.
See with what friendly calm I take your hand!
Let us be happy today!"

[130]

She turned her face aside—
It seemed, a moment, that she would have lied
Some intricate bewildering lie,—and then
She turned again
With frank pained eyes, unguarded and oppressed.
"I know that it is best
To tell you what I can," she said,—"to tell
What little can be told of this mad miserable
Heart that you know so small a portion of,—
A heart that cannot rest, not even in love . . ."

She paused; her eyes grew fathomless; but he
    broke
The silence, and spoke—
"Dear, dear, I love the tortured soul of you,
With curious fires fretted through and through;
The intricate homeless passions I divine
And all the longings that have been as wine
Drawing your spirit another way than mine.
And I ask nothing of this history.
Let it be mystery
To my dull brain—turn only and look at me."

And she, turning, with quiet voice and slow,
Said, as out of some depth of long-ago:

"Dear, have you hoped to find me
As in our sea-spell mood?
I cannot look behind me,
Stranger to certitude.
If happiness could but bind me,
Or beauty daze my blood! . . .

"Ah, will you understand? . . .
How can you know this strange hand in your hand,
Or think me other than more perverse, more vain,
     than shifting sand! . . .

     "I was utterly mad when you knew me
That first wild summer day.
I loved the swift winds that blew me
So wholly their way.
That hour in its curious fashion
Held wonderfully more
Of beautiful summer-born passion
Than any before.
I think that I loved you . . . but after,
What was I to do?
I drowned in renewals of laughter
My longing for you—
Seeking new flashes of summer
And singing and light . . .
But now my song has died; I have grown dumber
Than a desert at night.
I needed you, I wanted you,—but broken
Seem now my eager wings . . .
I scarcely understand what I have spoken
These troubled things."

     He answered her—"I think that now
You are tired by your baffling nights and days
Moving on barren ways.
I see your brow
More shadowy than it was.
But this will pass—

Pass, and the sun returning glimmer through
Its clouds to you.
Till then, a quiet pilgrim at your gate
Let me but wait."

"Is it so hard," she whispered, "to understand
That no old summer can return again?
My heart can never dwell in a belovèd land;
It wanders far away, in rapture or in pain,
And has its only strength in never seeking rest
For days or years on any human breast.
It must go crying
Up and down all the ways of the world, denied
That simple dying
Into mere peace by which alone it could be satisfied.
It cries for happiness, and each new wonder
In spite of distant thunder
Shines in the sunlight for it; and it takes:—
Then the earth shakes
And the skies darken about the sun
And the hour is done.
And onward down its labryinths my soul must move
         alone.

"You were my happiness: but now . . . My dear,
How you must hate me! . . . I am as one dead! . . .
Our madness has gone from me; I am here,
But my old joy is fled.
I am tired, tired, tired; the fevered day
Treads close upon the heels of fevered night;
I have thrown the sunshine and the stars away,
And whirled from vain delight to vain delight.
My dear, I am sorry . . . It is the spite of Fate . . .
But I am useless to you; you come too late!"

[133]

And he said—"Come away!
Somewhere there waits a new and fairer day
To set you free.
Let us go down into dear Italy,—
Florence, Ravenna, the groves of Sicily,—
And be together in each lovely spot
Until you have quite forgot
Your weariness and fever; these dead things
Shall seem to you but old imaginings.
This room, where I had thought to find
The Eden of my dreams, shall slip from mind
Wholly; and we shall be glad children again,
Playing beneath a sun that knows no pain
Nor any memory of the dismal rain
Of these dark northern cities, where too long
Your heart has stifled in labyrinths of wrong
Until, poor bird! it has forgot its song."

She listened; and there flickered on her face
A flush, a windy light; she raised her eyes
And searched his look, as though she hoped to trace
Beyond his words some gate of certainties,
Some spirit-portal flashing to her own
Its authenticity, to which her fears
Might flee secure. . . . Then the brief light was
        gone;
And forcing back to ebb a sudden tide of tears,
She only shook her head
Smilingly, gravely, and said—

"I am tired, tired, tired; no fresh rapture
Can wait for me. It has all been vain before! . . .
The butterflies I chase are broken by capture;
        [134]

The vista pales as I pass through each door.
I have ruined all the fair sweet things around me;
I have poisoned every flower that once I had;
All who have loved me in the end have found me
Cruel and base and profitless and mad.
Sole of them all, I mourn to see your going,
Yet have no power to hold you at my side.
I dreamed of you, once, by some magic growing
Into my friend, my lasting friend.   I lied
Then even to myself.   What friendship ever
Could cling to me, who am so little to trust? . . .
You will go from me: I desire it!   Never
Shall anything but hate spring from love's dust."

   She let him lift
His head from off her lap, and look her in the eyes.
He said— "I am not swift
To find a hatred ready to my hand:
Love stirs and cries
Even through this dusk I cannot understand,
Even through the silence of this desert land
Where we are wandering now.   My very dear,
Oh hear
From one who loves you, your own true report,
Of other sort.—

   "I think of you as of some jar
Moulded in days and lands afar
By an Egyptian potter, whom
Dawn, and the secrets of the tomb,
And desert-spaces, and the stars,
And doubt, and dreams, and life's fierce wars
So haunted that with curious hand

[135]

Around this urn he wove a band
Of intricate lovely tracery—
Illusive shapes that half-defy
One's vision:—spirits winged and proud—
Monsters as formless as a cloud—
High gateways of dull carven gold—
Sphinxes with cruel eyes, and cold
Pure water-nymphs. And many a face
Inscrutable and fair found place
Amid this pattern:—doubtful gleams
Of figures fainter than faint dreams—
The eyes of fear, the hands of lust,
The wings that flash above earth's dust.
And, finished, then he sealed inside
A perfume into which had died
Lotus and jasmine, honey-flower
And myrrh, from many a rose-hung bower
In Cashmere or in Samarkand.
And as its slender outlines stand
Before me now, my thoughts are lost
In marveling at the cruel cost
That made this beautiful tortured shape;
And from its perfumed heart escape
Such bitter-sweets of mystery
That I must love it till I die."

She laughed, with half a sob behind her tone.
"Oh dreamer! Had I known
That thus you held me, I would never have let
You see my face again,—never have met
Your mad, mad picture of me
With stark reality . . .
How shall I find a spell

[136]

To make me over into the miracle
That you have dreamed?
But, oh my dear! before you came, it seemed
That my prophetic fancy almost knew
What your wild hope would be . . .
—I will do anything that can set you free
From the unreal desire that witches you! . . .
I thought, at first, to meet you as you wanted—
Meet you with open arms and calling lips—
Trusting the picture that your heart has haunted
Would wane and die, under the slow eclipse
Of beauty in the torn storm of mere passion
Which still along my body your touch could wake.—
Aye, even now I can change,—in other fashion
Be with you, be your lover,—for your sake
Slaking the thirst, ridding you of this vision
Of you and me as white gods on a hill,—
Change love to calm and longing to derision . . .
If you choose, take me! . . . I will do your will" . . .

And a swift momentary brightness then
Swept through her eyes,
As though an authenticity, long lost to her, again
Was born out of the dust of old uncertainties
As Springs are born from snows, as flowers are born
      from dust—
Sweet, frank, unguarded,—like the tender and
      sacred breast
Of such a mother-love as can transcend the lust
Of its belovèd, offering sanctuary and rest . . .
Or like a desperate weary spirit, driven
To yield its outer walls, in last vain sacrifice
      given. . . .

Yet as she poured on him this light, there grew
A wider wonder in her face—
A flickering dream, a passion, that she too
Could by some magic word of his, some triumphing
     look, retrace
The labyrinth, and come swiftly again
To regions where old doubts of forest-lairs are
     slain,
And only splendors of wild wings sweep the sun-
     flooded plain. . . .

And he was silent, and on her shoulder
Laid his head, where the drooping dress
Down from the slender arm and throat had crept.
His heart was colder
Than snow, save that her delicate tenderness
Stirred in his soul so gently he could have wept.

And he said only—"No. . . .
It shall not be so." . . .

Her face paled, and a sudden weariness came
Into her eyes;
As though hope died then that his reckless flame
Of passion might with glorious surprise
Rekindle the grey embers: thus the last light went;
And she returned with tender voice to the old
     argument.

She said— "Oh are you sure?
Think not that if you suddenly went mad
It would be but a penance I must endure. . . .
I could be glad
And eager with your madness a little while—
My lips could smile

[138]

And my heart leap!—
And then, as out of sleep
We might hear echoes from a lovelier deep
That once we knew,—whose shores I can no longer
        keep. . . ."

  "It is enough; the dream is done;
The hour is over . . ." he said; and walked to where
Beyond the window the slow rain had begun
To blur the black night air
With greyness; and he watched the rivulets run
Down the dim street
Beneath the cold lamps' light,
And heard the hurrying feet
Of some late passer in the solitary night.

  And then at last he turned
Back to the circle where
The soft light burned
In rose and topaz on her cheek and hair.
And with the wind and rain
Monotonously astir
Outside the pane, quietly sat and endlessly talked
        with her.

  They talked quietly, slowly,
As friends for a long time parted,
As lovers whose loving was over. . . .
The hour grew tranquil and holy.
Once more she seemed the clear-hearted
Girl he had dreamed of as lover.
They were shut in by the sleeping
City around them wide,
Curious vigil keeping
Side by side. . . .

And in that pause, when the great stillness lay
Desert-like round the low dim words they said,
His vision swept to regions far away,
And a wide glow across his sight was shed.——
He seemed to see the whirling hosts of heaven,
Star after star, through endless voids of dark,
Each down its own gigantic orbit driven
Splendid and white and stark;
He saw the earth, that small dim troubled star,
Whirled in terrific dance amid the rest,
Swept by the tides' and by the seasons' war,
With earthquake-fires still threatening in its breast;
And on its surface in tumultuous droves
The passionate eager straining race of men,
Rapt in their labors, panting in their loves,
Dreaming, and dying into dreams again. . . .
And he beheld themselves:——bright spirits come
From earth's mysterious chemistry,——for a space
No longer dead, no longer blind and dumb,
Looking with human face on human face.
Here hand in hand and lip to eager lip
They might forget the irony of their doom,——
Possessed of happiness, before should slip
This one short hour into its waiting tomb.
For this was their hour, never to come again,
Never to sweep her eager heart and his
With these warm floods of human joy and pain
Mid candle-light and shadowy mysteries.
Strange life now for a moment filled their veins;
Strange death withheld its stroke a little while;
Now the world's chaos, its grim wars and pains,
Lay far apart; now they could meet, and smile,

And clasp each other,—lonely spirits lost
Amid time, space, that doomed them to defeat;
By hostile waves on this small island tossed
For this hour wholly sacred, wholly sweet,—
To touch each other wonderfully, know their hands,
Their brains, their bodies mingled in delight,—
Drawn from the limits of the farthest lands
To this one spot, to this immortal night!

But they,—he seemed to see,—
Who soon must die, never again to be
In any future time, on any other star
However far,
This passionate tragic human two
That this hour knew,—
They thus in the obscurity of pained thought
Desperately sought
Question and answer, and with intricate speech
Perturbed themselves, and each to each
Opposed vague subtleties of mind
And wandered blind. . . .
Ah, for a moment an overmastering hate
Rose in him against her whom he had late
Loved passionately well,—
Hate for her, that she could not, would not break
The spell
That bound them, and awake
Their own authentic ecstasies to leap
From this entangled nightmare-sleep,
And claim
Here on the very edge of death their April hour of
      flame.

He saw the sweetness
Of life, youth, love slip by them
Momently.
The ultimate completeness—
That did those powers deny them
Into which all things die. . .

XIX

"Sidonian lute!
Whose broken strings
Tremble in the darkness,
Echo in the darkness—
All other song grows mute
At your low murmurings,
Hushing my haunted keys
With dreams and silences."

XX

It was all like a dream to him, soon to be fled,
Those shadowy hours when they talked or were still.
But luminous flashes of what she said
Came back to him still.—

"My wonder-hour is over,
The hour in which I loved so recklessly.
And you,—dearest of all my April lovers,—
Think not too ill of me!
I, too, have dreamed,—would that I still were
    dreaming,
If only for your sake.
But round me lights are gleaming
Of icy dawn, and I have fallen awake. . . .

"My heart is wise: I cannot take your hand
And seek with you the quiet happy land
Of mere contented love that some hearts know.
Yet I am too distrustful now to go
Back to the glittering regions I have known
And be a spent leaf blown
In that unquiet gust
Of swift illusion and the moment's lust. . . .
My heart is as a stone! . . .
And in the universe I am alone,
And none can help me.   I must go
Toward some devotion that I do not know.
Strange! after all the seekings of the past
To find it is myself I need at last! . . .

"As if in nightmare-dreams, I now recall,
I have poised delicately lest I fall
From dangerous heights where I kept carnival—
Poised in a terrible dream of fear. . . .   Now I have
        fallen awake—and that is all. . . .

"Oh hate me if you must!
I have betrayed your happiness and trust.
But, dear, back to myself I could not choose but go.
And I pass from you lonelier than you know."

    And then it was, he said—
"If you were dead,
You who have made me happy and tortured me
With your inscrutable soul's perversity,—
Then I
Would weave around your name such golden song
As to no other woman might belong

[143]

Through all of history."
And she replied
Doubtfully, tenderly,—
"Would that I long ago had died!
For you, dear, I would die, save that the test
Would rob you of more rest
Than even my perversity of now.
Dear one, how painfully that vow
Would haunt your sleep forever!
No, for your sake, I will forbear to sever
The blue vein here; and though I cannot smile
With quite the madness that I once could use,
Surely I needs must choose
To save you from your oath, and live a little while!"

   The rain came down
Quietly, steadily, over the town.
They sat, silent; he dreaming of the lays
Whose coronal of praise
He would have woven for her were she dead.
Death-watch he seemed to keep—
For she had fallen asleep,
Resting upon his shoulder her quiet head.

XXI

"Faint-breathing music!
Beyond your peace are whispers
Haunting the darkness.
Far wandering music!
Into the shadows
Your chantings die."

[144]

XXII

Outside the window the rain slowly ceased;
And over all the housetops in the east
The mists divided slowly; the east grew grey;
And very far and low, a golden ray
Smote upward from the approaches of the day.
She opened her eyes; together they watched it grow,
And without speech thought of the long-ago
Dawn on the bosom of the summer sea.
Then again suddenly
And wearily
Her head drooped to his shoulder, and she said—
"I am tired, tired to dying.   Carry me
For once within your arms and lay me on my bed."

He lifted her slight lifeless form, and bore her
Down the long corridor to where, beneath
Its towering canopy, the white bed stood.
He lit the candle on the stand before her,
And as she lay in syncope, the sheath
Of gown took from her body, in such mood
As might a husband decking his dead spouse
For burial, and freed her sandaled feet,
And spread the great gold coverlet on the bed.
And in the emptiness of the silent house
Looked down upon the lids troubled and sweet,
And softly kissed the dark smooth drooping head.

She smiled a little and put out her arm,
Bare, beautiful; and drew him down, and kissed
His hair.
"You have put me safe beyond the reach of harm,"

[145]

She whispered. "I was so tired that a mist
Seemed to come down upon me unaware.
Good-bye!—I hope a long and last good-bye! . . .
And may you never hate me utterly!"

"Hate you!" . . . And then he felt
All barriers melt
Within him like an ice-bound river in Spring.
A sudden madness flamed in him; he knelt
Desperately by the bed,—then rose to fling
Himself upon it; with starved arms he pressed
Her long smooth body in a fierce embrace;
He buried his face
Against the delicate softness of her breast—
And cried—"You whom I love! what matters all
  the rest?
This, this is yours and mine,—this, this is best!"

And she stirred wildly in his tightening arms,—
At first as with alarms,—
Then, changing, clung with a fierce freed agony.
She clasped his head more closely to her side
And from the shaken depths of her being cried—
"Yes!— Yes!— Yes!—let it be!"

Then as he turned, dizzy with his delight,
Dreaming now at her side
To enter the golden hour of long ago,
He saw an ashen light
Sweep through her eyes,—bewildered, he saw her
  hide
Her face from him; and suddenly she cried—
"No, no, it cannot be! You will hate me—but go!
  . . . go! . . ."

[146]

And she sank back with drooping lids, and seemed
    to sleep, or slept;
While into the bright alien day, out of the silent
    house he crept. . . .

XXIII

. . . *"A mystery of music on the keys—*
A ghost of doubts and dreams and silences. . . .

"Over these keys, dim in the deeper darkness,
Slowly, hopelessly, silently wander my fingers,
Impotent now to awake an echo of you.
Chanting slowly, chanting with far-off voices,
Rises the host of implacable memories.
Into the darkness dies the unborn music;
And I remember the poignant you alone.

"This, strange and dear one,
This hour of memory is the only song
That I can ever make
For your pale coronal.
I would not do you the deep wrong
Of striving now to wake
Where grey rains fall
A measured artful voluntary of praise
Whose strains should die on the bewildered ears
Of those who thought you base
Or of a trivial worth.
For my own solace, thus I bring our days,
Our vain days, from their shroud of smiles and
    tears,

*Back for a little while to light the uncomprehending
      earth.*

  "Sidonian lute!
Still tremulous with music. . . .
Sidonian lute!" . . .

Rue des Vents

I

It was an old house; and there seemed to live
Along its mousey corridors still a gloom
Of lives long-cancelled. In my quiet room
Among my books, I could hear fugitive
Hesitant faint intrusions that withdrew
Before they had entered to my presence there.
The very light was thick, and on the stair
The darkness glowed and flickered. So I knew
I was at home here; for on every side
Beyond these walls, life to me thus had seemed
Always a hush where ancient voices hide—
A dusk where candles had but lately gleamed—
A masque of those who went and us who bide—
A dream that many another ghost has dreamed.

[149]

II

Here in the quiet chambers that I love
Evening falls gently; from the garden, cries
Of laughing children float; and high above
The old roofs, toward the western glow, there flies
A swallow from the south thus early come
To seek a summer that is still a dream.
The chestnut buds to woolly pods have grown
Green-lit beyond the window where I lean.
Summer is singing, and the night is still
With listening to that song; I too, oppressed
By some old faith in beauty, yield my will
To that which lights the gold lights of the west,—
And long for summer, though it come again
With dreams of beauty and with proof of pain.

III

This is the dusk-hour when for old love's sake
Ghosts in this garden might arise and move
Down vanished paths, and memories might awake
Out of the death that is so chill to love.
You whose old sins have in the later time
Become a legend perilous and sweet
With tragic whisperings of courtly rhyme,—
Lovely dead chatelaine!—are these your feet
That now across my silence slowly pace
Thrilling the darkness of this garden-close?
Turn! . . . No, this is no golden harlot's face,—
This is the bud that is not yet the rose,—
This is a ghost of things that never were,—
This is a child. The dusk grows sweet with her.

IV

Be wise, be wise, O heart forever seeking
A wine whose fever must the goblet break!
Let now the Sleeping Beauty lie a-sleeping;
Her lips could not speak sweeter did she wake.
Her dreams may last some happy moments still,
Before the dawn's first resonance of grey
Shall stir the east and, growing swiftly, fill
Her soul with joy and terror of the day.
Yet as the Sleeper lifts her quiet eyes
And to my troubled gaze their laughing glow
With loveliness and love of love replies,
I know that she has dreamed more than I know—
And lights outshining wisdom flush and start,
And summer sweeps wild wings across my heart.

V

Psyche! whose fairness of the rain-swept brow
And delicate breast and smooth unquiet hair
So long have filled my dreams,—what wonder now
That I again come and again find fair
The curve and color of these vestments worn
In mortal semblance for a little while?
Out of the far isles of the past reborn
You still keep, as in marble, this dim smile—
And I, the recurrent mortal lover, follow
Your pale recurrent dream of youthful love,
And seek as seeks in April's track the swallow
To trail your secret footsteps as you move;
Even like the swallow, little knowing why
Your look should light the earth and flush the sky.

[151]

VI

This day is all a greyness of dim rain.
Earth and the sky alike are wrapped in fold
Of the dim memory of some ancient pain,
Some wrong of bitter gods endured of old;
All grey and spent, save where I see you move
With lifted golden head and laughing eyes
And breast so delicate that no power but love
Could dwell there with his singing sorceries.
Proud little head, lifted amid the gloom!
Gay serious little heart, swift-running feet!
Into the shadowed broodings of this room
You bring the light of regions far and sweet;
Your laughter is a song, a golden beam
Out of the western rain-mist of my dream.

VII

When round you falls the silence of the dark,
Then golden caravels on magic seas
From you as from the world's edge might embark
To lands of light and isles of mysteries.
As on the slow tide of the violin
It seems that from the cool slope of your breast
My drowsed and gliding spirit's dreams might win
To unimagined silence of the west—
That beauty might so hush and daze the night
Love could transcend the bosom whence it sprang,
And fading on horizons of far flight
The song forget the summer lips that sang,
And into an undying summer soar
Where cloud and sky are one with sea and shore.

[152]

VIII

Your body's beauty is an air that blows
Out of some garden where the Spring has come—
Where never yet has faded any rose
And never any singing bird is dumb.
You are white waterfalls in piney woods
Touched by the freshness of October wind.
You are the slim young silver moon that broods
Over a dusk where lovers wander blind.
And how shall these eyes ever have their fill
Of you, alight with loveliness and love—
My starlight water, tremulous or still,
Across which music wakens as you move!
Over the floor laughing and white you pass. . . .
I see all April light that ever was.

IX

When the mad tempest of the blood has died
And sleep comes on, still I am half aware
Of the long sloping music of your side,
And windy light is round me with your hair.
I move through dusks between the day and night
Where night and day and vision intertwine;
The breast of Her who was the gods' delight
Touches a cheek I vaguely know is mine.
Doubt and believing mingle while there stirs
Your hand that wakens mine out of its dream;
Hope knows not what is hers, nor Memory hers,
Amid the marble curves that change and stream;
And only Beauty, through dim lights, can claim
These hours that have no time or place or name.

[153]

X

O happy heart, O heart of loveliness!
Against the morning you lift up your face,
And smile against the morning's smile, no less
Beautiful than her beauty; and the grace
Of her long-limbed and sweet processional hours
Is but attendant on your morning laughter.
Trailing her wreaths and scattering her flowers,
Where your light footsteps go, she follows after—
Follows your feet with sunlight. . . . Till we are
Silent again and lonely, where there rise
Dark evening trees, over them one great star,
While other stars come slowly to the skies—
And hand in hand, where the world goes to rest
I am lost in wonder, and silent is your breast.

XI

Your beauty shall not save you from despair
In after-days when life is not so sweet
Along the garden-paths. That you were fair
And well-belovèd, can it ease your feet
Down through the dark upon whose edge I stand
And see the shadows deepening on ahead
Even to the borders of the empty land
Where beauty ends and all the dreams are dead?
Child! drink the sunlight of this perfect hour
Which makes a slender blossom of your breast!
Time has gone dreaming, that your heart may
    flower;
And while he sleeps, be happy. That is best;
And laugh in triumphing beauty, even at one
Who in each flower sees flowers that now are gone.

[154]

XII

Here at my window, in the waning light
Of afternoon, with serious bended head
You labor at a letter; as you write,
I wonder—can words say what should be said?
I wonder if the misspelled lines can hold
Anything of this rapt and dreaming face,
The delicate brow, the carven wavy gold,
The white neck bent in dim abstracted grace?
That lad in battle to whom your message flies—
I in my madness wish that he could share
This hour.   No inky page of your replies
Could speak to him as speaks this gold-shot hair
To me who linger—near, yet more afar
Than you, boy, can be, wheresoever you are.

XIII

Since beauty holds no lease of settled date,
And youth has tenure but while roses blow,
And mortal hope must yield to mortal fate,
And every dream that comes must one day go—
Since these most lovely phantoms cannot be
Companions in the grey years that confess
Wild love to hold life's chiefest sovereignty,
Yet must without it seek for happiness—
Then let the autumn of the soul become
Transfigured with its own appropriate hues;
As, in high pageant, when the flowers are dumb
Old forests lift the splendor earth must lose,
And hills with solemn foliage of the fall
Outvaunt the spring, in phantom festival.

[155]

XIV

Go by! but go not lightly; as you pass
Send back such gleam as the departing sun
Pours down the hill-slopes where the fading grass
Turns to a path of gold.   The day is done
And evening stars come on.   Yet you shall rise
Tomorrow to a world once more complete.
And green shall be the valleys to your eyes
And fair shall be the paths before your feet.
But as you go your way across the earth,
Look back sometimes, belovèd, and recall
I taught you love and laughter at their worth;
And of the bitterness, I knew it all
And would have spared you, had the power been
       mine . . .
Dreams, dreams again!   There is no anodyne.

XV

Birds that are beautiful and sing in the sun
Fly southward when the summer day is done.
Oh may the fountains of the golden south
Be worthy of your delicate thirsting mouth!
Oh may the magic of the tropic isles,
Where the great palm trees lift their tufted crests,
Answer the light and music of your smiles
And may the waves curl gently round your breasts.
Southward as goes the swallow to the sun
May you go ever till the race be run—
And at the end, may Time, whose terrible feet
Behind your lovely flying steps are fleet,
Strike with swift mercy, that your final breath
Be ignorant, as your glad lips were, of death.

[156]

Don Quixote

They told Don Quixote he was old and dazed,
Ill-born, a pauper, not a knight at all,
A thing to make the very crows amazed
With the grotesqueness of his spectacle.
I think his words of answer spoke but part
Of his defence against the worldly crew;
I think great lights were flashing in his heart
Whereof he told not, and they never knew.
I think he saw all that they saw, and more—
The gaunt and tattered knight, the sorry frame;
But cared not, knowing that his bosom bore
The living embers of a vanished flame,
And that his memory guarded now alone
The history of a beauty that was gone.

"However," said the Bachelor Carrasco,—
"Some souls there be, reading your history,
Who wish the author had not numbered so
The bafflements that were your misery
And foil, most noble knight!"   But Sancho, wise,
Spoke that thick candor which is half his zest:
"In these falls lies the history; all were lies
With these left out; and truth, gadzooks, is best!"
"Aye, truth to mortal eyes!" the old knight said,
"But such a truth might well have been let go.
Things that light not the living or the dead
Are of small profit for our brains to know.
Prove that the real Æneas was a knave,
And have you then stirred Virgil in his grave?"

Don Quixote died a sane man; at his bed
The curate and the barber marvelling stood,
Admiring his new wisdom as he said
Clear words, abjuring in his dying mood
All of the far adventurings, cursing all
The old enchantments, casting out all Fays
Of mad romances that had sounded call
So clarion-like to his knight-errant days.
Thus drew the high strange tragedy to its close;
Thus the great dupe and dreamer ebbed, was gone.
Madmen end ill, as everybody knows;
The barber and the curate, they lived on.
Poor knight! God viewed thee with a jealous eye,
Since mad and great He would not let thee die.

Dearest of all the heroes! peerless knight,
Whose follies sprang from such a generous blood!
Young, young must be the heart that in thy fight
Beholds no ghost of its own servitude.
Young, or else darkened, is the eye that sees
No image of its own fate in thy quest.
The windmills and the swine—by such as these
Is shaped the doom of those we love the best.
Belovèd knight! La Mancha's windows gleam,
Across the plain time makes so chill and grey,
With thy light only.   Still thy flambeaux stream
In pomp of one who on his destined day
Put up his spear, his knightly pennon furled,
And died of the unworthiness of the world.

Great ghost! who in the autumn of the year,
When through gaunt branches terrible winds that
        blow
Seem whispering to us, seem more close and dear
Than all the human voices that we know—
Great ghost! who loved uncomprehended space
And were so fevered with immortal time,
Who dreamed that heaven lit up one chosen face,
And trusted fantasies crowded into rhyme—
Be not too far from us; come, at the pane
Flatten your pale face and look in on us:
We also are of those who live in vain;
Like you we are noble and ridiculous;
Like you we haunt a savage autumn night
In dizzy errantries of lonely flight.

On Tides of Time

I

On tides of time that fluctuate to and fro—
From deep to shallow, from rock-shore to deep—
The waters sway; we with them.   All we know
Is the dim surface of a sea asleep.
Fierce tides preceding this mild planet's birth
Have set the measure of each season's mood;
They rule the day-and-night pulse of the earth
No surer than the pulses of our blood.
On tides of time we, drifting to and fro,
Committed to a helpless bark, are borne—
One day, by gentle winds; then, tempests blow
Their devastation and all sails are torn
And the great fishes wait, hungry, below—
None else to welcome us, and none to mourn.

[160]

II

It is not known; so certify it not
With august oaths and pious mysteries.
Before all prophets, prophets now forgot
Spoke different truth; and others before these.
Sun rises and sun sets; the seasons pass;
The child is born, and grows, and lives, and dies;
Sometimes unearthly beauty lights the grass
And sometimes storms fill the whole darkened skies.
There are such days as make men wish to live
Forever in their unreceding light;
And there are hours that drive the fugitive
To clutch the kind robe of eternal night.
And where beyond these things man's faith has
    flown,
Wonder!—but warrant not. It is not known.

III

The old? We are the old. And now we know
How the fresh mirror dims with passing time.
Not for us rise the carven gods, or blow
The haunting musics; not for us the rhyme
Of dreaming singers, nor the lights that drift
Faintly through dusks, nor hopes that once had
    stung.
We mumble down our pathway, making shift
To mock the unstable visions of the young.
We mock them, tell them they shall yet be wise;
We point and peer at clods and stones and trees
Beyond where Helen, living, past their eyes
Drifts white, and Jason breasts the darkening seas;
And flout our early love-songs, vain and cold
To eyes so certain and to hearts so old.

[161]

IV

Because of this we die; because of this
Wise Nature calls us toward the facts we trust,
And clears her stage for later mysteries
By yielding us the tangible couch of dust
Where we shall doubt no more, being quite content
With the one kindly ultimate certitude,
Far from the minstrel-paths down which we went
Where new hopes waken and new dreamers brood.
We, silent in our vested sepulchers,
Trouble no more at sense or daze of those
Within whose eyes the great illusion stirs
And through whose hearts the joy of beauty blows
Its flickering light and music from the deep.
They have the light and music; we, the sleep.

V

This strange importuning! This dull desire
Claiming a pageant past its mortal day!
Certain it is the earth shall end in fire
Or ice, and our long toil be swept away
Or pass so changed it bears no likeness then
To that creation whose each line we proved.
The statue's beauty and the deeds of men
Have term, though nobly planned, superbly loved.
Patience, my soul! whose indiscriminate greed
Must grasp all measure or rejoice in none!
The wise man takes the treasures of his need,
Content to glow his small day in the sun,
Nor bids the high and happy hour profess
Its only warrant is its lastingness.

[162]

VI

Here in the daylight, where the singing mood
Can sometimes light our lips, and sometimes come
Love's ancient musics chanting down our blood,
And sometimes stars wheel out when nights are
    dumb—
Where hands may touch, and minds assault or fold
Each others' or the world's most foul or bright,
And hear the story of old kingdoms told,
And onward dream through time's unchartered
    night—
Here where a glory of imagining thought
May light with blush the Galatean stone,
And the heart's picture of the thing it sought
For all the baffled bitter years atone—
Lordly possessor of the far and near!
Here is our home; our stage of dreams is here.

The Middle Years

Women in mirrors, we are told, may see
The wings of beauty as, with anxious eye,
They trace the legend of mortality
And day by day watch the old magic die.
In different wise, I in my glass behold
The flight of what no springtime can replace,
And start with terror of things grim and old
When chance confronts me with my mirrored
    face—
Where the long seasons have engraven deep
So many an epitaph of satiric rhyme
And sent so many a flaming light to sleep
And branded immortality so with time,
That where a stranger might see youth alone
I view the ghosts of things that now are gone.

This is the burden of the middle years:
To know what things can be, or not be, known;
To find no sunset lovely unto tears;
To pass not with the swallow southward flown
Toward far Hesperides where gold seas break
Beyond the last horizon round strange isles;
To have forgot Prometheus on his peak;
To know that pilgrim-miles are only miles.
Then death seems not so dreadful with its night
That keeps unstirred a veil of mystery.
Then no acclaimed disaster can affright
Him who is wise in human history
And finds no godhead there to earn his praise
And dreads no horror save his empty days.

Not all my will can change this casque of bone
That predetermines what each thought must be;
And I have learned to bear with these my own
Enforced defects and doomed futility,
And with reproach no longer rack a skull
Whose rigid plan, conditioned long ago,
Left such low arches for the beautiful
To pour its summer light through. Now I know
Somewhat the measure of what may be done
And may not by this child of a dark race,
Who in the long processions of the sun
Today for a brief moment takes his place.
I bid him bear his banner with the rest,
Nor too much blame the dusk that haunts his breast.

[165]

I can more tranquilly behold the stars
Than once I could.   Their alien majesty
Awakes in me no longer desperate wars
Against their far indifference circling by.
For I too have my orbit, and intent
Upon its rondure I no less than they
Decline the test of warlike argument.
They go their several ways; I go my way.
Nothing of all my hopes have they denied,
Nor do I storm against them as of old.
We pass, the sovereigns of an equal pride.
Some day shall I be dead and they be cold.
Until that hour, untroubled in our flight
We seek our own paths through the spacious night.

It thunders in the west, where the clouds roll
Ominously; and as the winds arise
Once more the lightnings cry out to my soul.
How often have I stood with passionate eyes
On some bare hilltop whence the miles of plain,
By sudden flashes torn forth from their sleep,
Were for an instant scrutable, till again
Atlantis-like they sank to oceans deep!
And such is life's true image: no clear day
On plain-lands luminous and defined and grave—
But a wild dusk where flashes, far away,
Swiftly illumine shores that from the wave
Are for a moment lifted, soon to be
Merged once again in the concealing sea.

What good, I ask myself, what fortunate thing
Amid so many evils that we taste,
Do these strange years of middle-passage bring,
Where thief and rust and moth have so made
 waste?
And as I count them over one by one—
Patience and prudence and more generous
 thought—
I see none here to match the great gifts gone
Nor any fit atonement time has brought.
—Save perhaps one: the calm and certain will
Whose baffled purpose still relentless goes
Across the world, unconquerable still,
Seeking the unknown goal that well it knows—
Like a bleak eagle that with blinded eye
Drives on its way across the wind-swept sky.

Personalities and Diversions

TO A GIRL SINGER

I sit beside you, or I watch you walk
Across some room or wander down a street;
I notice that your talk is idle talk
And that you have pale hair and little feet;
I see you have a swift and troubled smile,
And odd secretive glimmerings in your eyes—
And I turn from you, terrified by the guile
Of this suave simple exquisite disguise.
For I have been too shaken by the power
Of what in depths of solitude you have sung
To prize your friendship in a human hour.
I still remember that your spirit flung
Certain gigantic shadows against the sky—
And I have doubts of your mortality!

TABLES

Once the altar was sacred;
But now, I think, it is the table.

For across tables
Go the words, the looks, the blinding flashes of
    thought
That are truly the race's history.
Fellow-lovers and fellow-poets
Lean their arms on these white surfaces,
And bending forward oblivious above the scattered
    silver,
Enkindle each other's souls.
I have never got from a pulpit
What I have got from tables.
I have never been so stirred in the greenwood
As at these curious urban trysting-places.
Nor do I think that heaven itself
Will wholly answer to my need,
Unless in obscure streets and squares and avenues
And purlieus outlying the Pillared Place
There are little cafés
Where across tables
Blessèd angels whisper wonderful and incredible
    secrets to one another.

FANTASY FOR A CHARMING FRIEND

This goblet is a little loving-cup.
I raise it to my lips, and where you kissed
There lurks a certain sting that I have missed
In nectars more laboriously put up.
Your hair is hissing startled golden sounds
Through gratings of your little cage of lies;
And I can read a promise in your eyes
As sunset fades across the coffee-grounds.
Yet vain the hope we shall collaborate
In this or that disorder, bad or worse;
For I but chase off flies with bits of verse,
While you resolve the curls of Time and Fate;
And though our path be circular or straight,
This is no Roman chariot, but a hearse.

You have, my love, mosquitoes in your eyes
That circle in a little cloud, and sting,
And make me mad for almost anything
That could provide indelicate surprise.
Here with the rag-bag of our destinies
Emptied upon the floor, in a small ring
We, sorting over pieces, softly sing;
And I sing music, love; and you sing lies.
O pampered darling on whose velvet knees
The Sphinx of carven ages lolls and purrs!
There shall be other æons after these
In which to whet those silver claws of hers.
Wherefore I do entreat you, an you please,
Not to disturb my whited sepulchers.

You are a minx, a marten, and a mouse:
Come in, for my menagerie is wide.
Though bed, or tree-nest, or wainscoting-house
You shall prefer, all lodgings I provide.
For I am very fearful you may choose
By stealth a secret triumph here to win;
So I make choice of what is least to lose,
And lest you draw me out, I draw you in.
Enter! and in these old halls take your rest
Or whatsoever else you choose to take.
You have a curious brain, a delicate breast—
I make you welcome here for either's sake.
Play on, my love, at being little sphinx,
While I set chairs for marten, mouse, and minx.

Yet, lest with too much taunting of the gods
They should grow angry that I torture so
Their beauty into devious periods,
I will speak truth one moment ere I go.
I will confess that loveliness has stirred
Like a long music through me many a time
When all my courts and fountains with some word
Of yours were echoing in a silver rhyme—
That when the apes and peacocks all have done
With prancing in the portico, there shall be
A recollection, safe from sun to sun,
Within the dark high-vaulted halls of me—
And one tall window, dearer than the rest,
Whose prospect is your open golden west.

LINES TO THEODORE DREISER

There were gilded Chinese dragons
And tinkling danglers of glass
And dirty marble-topped tables
Around us, that late night-hour.
You ate steadily and silently
From a huge bowl of chop-suey
Of repellent aspect;
While I,—I, and another,—
Told you that you had the style neither of Sir
    Thomas Browne
Nor of Walter Pater.

And our reproaches were perfectly true. . . .
But you continued to occupy yourself
With your quarts of chop-suey;
Your unresponsive dullness was a gloom
Around our bright heroic wisdom.
Then—somehow you reminded me
Of nothing so much as of the Knitting Women
Who implacably counted stitches while the pride of
    France
Went up to death.
    Tonight I am alone—
A long way from that Chinese restaurant,
A long way from wherever you are.
And I find it difficult to recall to my memory

The image of your large, laboring, inexpressive
    face.
For I have just turned the last page
Of a book of yours—
A book large and superficially inexpressive—like
    yourself.
It has not, any more than the old ones,
The style of Browne or of Pater.
But now there are passing before me
Interminable figures in tangled procession—
Proud or cringing, starved with desire or icy,
Hastening toward a dream of triumph, fleeing from
    a dream of doom—
Passing—passing—passing—
Through a world of shadows,
Through a chaotic and meaningless anarchy,
Under heavy clouds of terrific gloom
Or through ravishing flashes of knife-edged
    sunlight—
Passing—passing—passing—
Their heads haloed with immortal illusion—
The terrible and beautiful, cruel and wonder-laden
    illusion
Called life.

KING OF SALAMANDERS

To John Cowper Powys

Old salamander basking in the fire,
Winking your lean tongue at a coal or two,
Lolling amid the maelstroms of desire,
And envying the lot of none or few—
Old serpent alien to the human race,
Immune to poison, apples, and the rest,
Examining like a microbe each new face
And pawing, passionless, each novel breast—
Admirer of God and of the Devil,
Hater of Heaven, Purgatory, and Hell,
Skeptic of good, more skeptic yet of evil,
Knowing the sick soul sounder than the well—
We mortals send you greetings from afar—
Now very like a human being you are!

Impenetrably isolate you stand,
Tickling the world with a long-jointed straw.
Lazy as Behemoth, your thoughts demand
No cosmic plan to satisfy your maw;
But as the little shining gnats buzz by
You eat the brightest and spit out the rest,
Then streak your front with ochre carefully
And dance, a Malay with a tattooed breast.
There are no sins, no virtues left for you,
No strength, no weakness, no apostasy.
You know the world, now old, was never new,
And that its wisdom is a shameless lie.
So in the dusk you sit you down to plan
Some fresh confusion for the heart of man.

Lover of Chaos and the Sacred Seven!
Scorner of Midas and St. Francis too!
Wearied of earth, yet dubious of Heaven,
Fain of old follies and of pastures new—
Why should the great, whose spirits haunt the void
Between Orion and the Northern Wain
Make you their mouthpiece? Why have they
employed
So brassed a trumpet for so high a strain?
Perhaps, like you, they count it little worth
To pipe save for the piping; so they take
You, weak, infirm, uncertain as the earth,
And down your tubes the thrill of music wake.
Well, God preserve you! and the Devil damn!—
And nettles strew the bosom of Abraham!

AN OUTRAGEOUS PERSON

To Floyd Dell

God forgive you, O my friend!
For, be sure, men never will.
Their most righteous wrath shall bend
Toward you all the strokes of ill.

You are outcast—Who could bear,
Laboring dully, to behold
That glad carelessness you wear,
Dancing down the sunlight's gold?

Who, a self-discovered slave,
As the burdens on him press,
Could but curse you, arrant knave,
For your crime of happiness?

All the dogmas of our life
Are confuted by your fling,
Taking dullness not to wife,
But with wonder wantoning.

All the good and great of earth,
Prophesying your bad end,
Sourly watch you dance in mirth
Up the rainbow, O my friend!

ALCIBIADES TO A JEALOUS GIRL

Slender one, white one,
You seem to marvel
With troubled brows
That I can waver
Even for a moment
In curious choice
Between you and the wine-cup.

Listen, little one,
Listen, white one,
While I speak truth
To those small hidden
Delightful ears of yours.—
You bring a goddess
Down to earth
For tryst with me;
But the wine-cup,
Oh the wine-cup
Elevates me to be one
Of the company of all the gods!

CAFÉ SKETCH

To Donald Evans

In a remote alcove
Sits tonight
One whom I know to be a poet—
A great poet, but keyed
In a pitch that is neither the world's
Nor that of other poets.
Once he was a keen knife of spirit
Stabbing dull hearts;
But now he is wearied out wholly
Save for the brief renascence of the midnight hour.
Across the table
A pale, flame-lipped, very exquisite girl
Looks at him with inscrutable eyes.
Then, as his lips move—
Then, as he leans forward—
I see, I divine, that he says:

"Light-foot whisperer over the dark abysses!—
Beautiful breast
Never to be forgotten!—
Evilly have you worked upon me!
Now the orange floods of the afternoon

[179]

And the watery green depths of the midnight,
The vestal dawn
And the scarlet screaming dawn
Flicker with your passage!

"Glittering, gay, fantastic, unhappy child—
You seem as old as the oldest sin of the world
And as young as its newest rapture.
You are to me fresh April,
And the last days of October,—
Honey, and myrrh,—
The delicate dusk, and the stark dawn-light.
I have expected you a long time
With wonder and with terror;
And now, with your kiss upon my lips,
I await the miracle to result—
Corruption, or transfiguration."

And she, having listened
With inscrutable eyes and lips that were motionless,
Drank the champagne in her glass,
And looked curiously into the distance;
While he went on:

"You have brought me a lost wonder
And stirred in me a romance
I had forgotten.

"Now I again see landscapes
Clothed in their rightful mystery,
And the dusk is again holy,
And food is again sweet.

"Now I am alive
Who was dead."

But her lips did not move,
Not even with a smile.
And then he said,
While the violins sang with him:

"Lovely child—on your breast
Could a head find snowy rest?
Could the dizzy pulses cease
And the madness take release?
Yes! Yes! that I know—
For I dreamed it long ago. . . .
But, child, on what breast
Shall *your* head find rest?"

She turned her eyes away from him,
And her lips were as quiet as lilies. . . .
Red lilies of a garden in Cashmere. . . .
Then the dancers fluttered out
Into the pools of the spot-light. . . .
And she smiled.

QUESTIONING A LADY

"Yes, he was my first lover.   Did I love him?
No, not as you and I make use of words.
Outside his world, below him or above him,
Remained the silences that are love's accords.
His infinite curiosity too much pried
Into that darkness which was mine alone.
Sometimes I wished that I had merely died
Before I let him think I was 'his own.'
I am nobody's own; I am a being
Simple, perplexed, unhappy, like the rest;
Toward beauty turning and from boredom fleeing.
No special secret hides in this my breast.
Let us this dubious inquiry now give over. . . .
Or are you not my friend,—only my lover?"

EPITAPH FOR A BAD GIRL

Her heart, born eager, generous and just,
Failed to perceive the sordidness of lust.
She thought it lovely, and she made it so.
Because of this, about the world there go
A score of men who writhe in generous shame
When hot or icy lips whisper her name.

They turn to silence when her name is spoken.
Not glove or garter is produced as token.
They look with empty, hurt, remembering eyes
Upon a world so good, so chaste, so wise.

THE VILLAGE ARTIST

He cursed the church, he drank much gin,
He followed wenches by the score.
He was a man of utter sin.
Our matrons turned him from the door.

He made a rainbow glory grow
As if old streets were regions new.
Forgotten loves of long ago
Touched an old woman whom he drew. . . .

He died at last, of too much gin . . .
We are a Christian folk, and we
Treasure, forgiving of his sin,
His pictures for posterity.

LINES FOR TWO REBELS

Why does all of sharp and new
That our modern days can brew
Culminate in you?

This chaotic age's wine
You have drunk—and now decline
Any anodyne.

On the broken walls you stand,
Peering toward some stony land
With eye-shading hand.

Is it lonely as you peer?
Do you never miss, in fear,
Simple things and dear—

Half-remembered, left behind?
Or are backward glances blind
Here where the wind

Round the outposts sweeps and cries—
And each distant hearthlight dies
To your restless eyes? . . .

I too stand where you have stood;
And the fever fills my blood
With your cruel mood.

Yet some backward longings press
On my heart: yea, I confess
My soul's heaviness.

Me a homesick tremor thrills
As I dream how sunlight fills
My familiar hills.

Into that profound unknown,
Where the earthquake forces strown
Shake each pilèd stone,

Look I; and exultance smites
Me with joy; the splintered heights
Call me with fierce lights.

But a piety still dwells
In my bones; my spirit knells
Solemnly farewells

To safe halls where I was born—
To old haunts I leave forlorn
For this perilous morn. . . .

Yet I come; I cannot stay;
Yours and mine the terrible day;
Yours and mine the unknown way;

Where you go, I go.   But me
Mock not lightly.   I come free—
But with agony.

IMMORTALS IN EXILE

Beneath a goblin yew-tree's shade,
When autumn night was furled,
I saw them gather who have made
The history of the world—

Those great obscure momentous souls
Whom fame does not record—
Whose impulse still our fate controls
With deathless deed or word.

There walked the postman from whose face
No shock the smile could oust,
Who lost, beyond our power to trace,
The sketch of Lessing's "Faust."

There came the snivelling servant-maid
With injured peevish look
Who on the lagging fire-coals laid
Carlyle's long-labored book.

One plodded by whose father-love,
Surmounting all defeats,
Had made a first-class plumber of
A boy who was a Keats.

[187]

And ambling amiably along
The Man from Porlock strode,
Whose visit broke the wizard song
Of Kubla Khan's abode.

And many more, to me unknown,
Gathered beneath the trees—
Men who perhaps down wells have thrown
Plays of Euripides,

Or sold some budding Shakespeare drink,
Or shut in cells some Blake,
Or forced some Shelley to death's brink
For true religion's sake.

I heard them say: "We are oppressed,
Damned by a cruel wrong—
We who have always meant the best
And have meant nothing long—

"Most cruelly damned, to such degree
That sinners, faring well
In warmth and good society,
Eject us even from Hell.

"Hence are we forced to seek on earth
The form of mortal wight;
And entering at the gates of birth,
Resume our ancient might."

WALPURGISNACHT

The fiery coals were glowing.
The winter howled outside.
We were alone together
With nothing left to hide.

She let slip from her shoulders
Her furs and finery
And stood before the hearth-glow
And made her body free.

And I too dropped my garments
And in the glow we stood
Shameless and passionless as death,
So ghostly was our mood.

We looked upon each other;
We touched; we moved apart.
There was a silence over us,
A hunger of the heart

For some undreamed communion,
Some ecstasy of pain . . .
She smiled: we donned our clothes and went
Out to the streets again.

SONG OF A VERY SMALL DEVIL

He who looks in golden state
Down from ramparts of high heaven,
Knows he any change of fate,
It must be of evil given—
He perhaps shall wander late
Downward through the luminous gate.

He who makes himself a gay
Dear familiar of things evil—
In some deepest tarn astray—
Close-companioned of the Devil—
He can nowhere turn his way
Save up brighter slopes of day.

Plight it is, yet clear to see.
Hence take solace of your sinning.—
As ye sink unfathomably
Heaven grows ever easier winning.
Therefore ye who saved would be,
Come and shake a leg with me!

LOREINE: A HORSE

She lifted up her head
With the proud incredible poise
Of beauty recovered
From the Mycenaean tombs.

She opened her nostrils
With the wild arrogance
Of life that knows nothing
Except that it is life.

Her slender legs
Quivered above the soft grass.
Her hard hooves
Danced among the dandelions.

Her great dark eyes
Saw all that could be seen.
Her large lips
Plucked at my coat-sleeve.

All the wisdom of the prophets
Vanished into laughter
As Loreine lifted her small foot
And pawed the air.

All the learning of the sages
Turned to ribald rubrics
When that proud head
Looked at a passing cloud.

And so, amid this godless
God-hungry generation,
Let us, my friends, take Loreine
And worship her.

She would demand nothing,
Nor would she utter thunders.
She is living, and real,
And she is beautiful.

Asian Oracles

KORIUSAI SPEAKS

Let whoso will take sheets as wide
As some great wrestler's mountain-back.
Space cannot hide
His lack.

Take thou the panel, being strong.
'Tis as a girl's arm fashioned right—
As slender and divinely long
And white.

That tall and narrow icy space
Gives scope for all the brush beseems.
And who shall ask a wider place
For dreams?

It is an isle amid the tides—
A chink wherethrough shines one lone star—
A cell where calms of heaven hide
Afar.

One chosen curve of beauty, wooed
From out the harsh chaotic world,
Shall there in solitude
Be furled.

The narrow door shall be so strait
Life cannot vex, with troubled din,
Beauty, beyond that secret gate
Shut in.

Lo! I will draw two lovers there,
Alone amid their April hours,
With lines as drooping and as fair
As flowers.

I will make Spring to circle them
Like a faint aureole of delight.
Their luminous youth and joy shall stem
The night.

And men shall say: Behold! he chose,
From Time's wild welter round him strown,
This hour; and paid for its repose
His own.

IRISES

Whence flows this stream
In which the iris stems
Amid their sword-like leaves
Rise in pale purple?
From what far hills
Comes the cool water
Here swirling
Into eddies and currents?

"This water comes
From my far homeland—
From the far hills
Where as a child
I walked the crests
And saw the sunrise
That promised glories
To my waiting heart.

"But now my days
Are empty of glories;
And my nights are troubled
With the passion of men.
Life passes by me
Like the passing water
Of the cool stream
Coming from afar.

[195]

"Last night there came
Unto my dwelling,—
Open to so many
That all may come,—
A silent painter,
A man of dreaming.
And when he left me
In the cold dawn
I slept, and dreamed
Strangely of the far hills
Misted at sunrise
That I once had known,—
Of my old country,
The land of iris,—
And I awoke
And was at peace."

DREAM OF A CHINESE LANDSCAPE

Mists are rolling
Over the grey mountains,
Over the quiet waters
And marshy shores,—
Rolling up into valleys
Where pagodas rise,—
Rolling over slopes
Along whose crests
Monasteries dream.
Wild geese soar
Above the marshes
In downward flight—
In flight from unknown shore
To unknown shore.
Over all
Mists are swaying.

The shadowy bridge
And wandering roadway,
The dark gnarled tree by the road
And the pale tree afar,
Are touched with doubtful mists
Or emergent from lifting mists,—
Trembling in mist; born of mist; shadows. . . .

O mountains, shores, and streams!
Beautiful transient illusion!
Mortal world, dream world,
Vanishing into mist, into mist only!

[197]

FIGURE OF A GIRL BY HARUNOBU

Ye winds that somewhere in the West—
In gulfs of sunset, isles of rest,
Rise dewy from prenatal sleep
To strew with little waves the deep—
Surely it is your breath that stirs
These fluttering gauzy robes of hers!

Come whence ye may, I marvel not
That ye are lured to seek this spot.
Your tenuous scarcely-breathèd powers
Sway not the sturdier garden-flowers,
And had unmanifest gone by
Save that she feels them visibly.

O little winds, her little hands
In time with tunes from fairy-lands
Are moving; and her bended head
Knows nothing of the long years sped
Since heaven more near to earth was hung,
And gods lived, and the world was young.

[198]

Peace folds her in its deeps profound;
Her shy glance lifts not from the ground;
And through this garden's still retreat
She moves with tripping silver feet
Whose trancèd grace,where'er she strays,
Turns all the days to holy days.

Come! Let us softly steal away.
For what can we, whose hearts are grey,
Bring to her dreaming paradise?
A chill shall mock her from our eyes;
A cloud shall dim this radiant air;
Come! for our world is otherwhere.

But O ye little winds that blow
From golden islands long ago
Lost to our searching in the deep
Of dreams between the shores of sleep—
Ye shall her happy playmates be,
Fluttering her robes invisibly.

THE OLD MEN'S TALE

*(From "The History of the Three Kingdoms" by
Lo Kuan Chung)*

Green are the hills as in far times forgotten.
But past them flows a river to the eastward
That journeys ever and that changes ever—
A ceaseless current.

The gifted and the great have known its windings,
And drifted with them past our farthest vision.
And good and evil and defeat and conquest
Down that stream vanish.

We, the old men, white-haired and full of leisure,
Quietly tend our little isle of waters,
Spending our days in the calm life of fishers
With the flood round us.

We look upon the silent moon of Autumn;
We feel the coolness of the Spring's light breezes;
And with a jar of gleeful wine between us
We meet together;

And all the past, gone down the eternal river,
And all the present, floating on its bosom,
Are to us but a pleasant tale remembered,
Told in the twilight.

BRAHMA

I Am; and yet I never was.
I Am; yet I shall never be.
I Am Not; yet my pulses pass
From first to last eternity.

Brahma am I, and Vishnu too,
And Siva—maker, savior, flame
Of ruin.   Can thy mind then view
Me who am Three and still the same?

I shatter cities in their might
And shape soft flowers of their clay.
I break the hundred towers of night
To build therewith the dome of day.

Brahma am I; I shape all things
Whereof the wisest mouth can tell.
I fashion from the mould of kings
The butterfly.   And it is well.

Vishnu am I; it is my will
The stone should lie where once it fell,
The sun still shine to warm the hill,
The heart still hope.   And it is well.

Siva am I; with scathing fire
I sweep the worlds like wind of Hell.
With all its web of vain desire
Creation falls.   And it is well.

Thus through the courts of starry space
I who am all, who am the Three,
Cast on the dark of time and place
The light of Mine Eternity.

THE WILD DUCK

The heron rises and circles;
The wild duck steadily flies
Past the shadowy lake and marshes
Toward the yellow western skies.

The ripples murmur and travel
Outward in golden lines.
A wild duck flaps from the marshes
And rises over the pines.

Shadows sink on the woodland
Mistily deepening more.
A wild duck flies toward the sunset.
A wild duck lifts from the shore.

I am lone in this land of marshes;
I wander its silent streams,
Where I hear but the wild duck calling
And see but the yellow gleams.

Dark comes on the quiet waters.
The pine-trees sink in haze.
Only the west is lighted
With ruin of many days.

Only the rushes murmur
On the water's mirror breast,
As a wild duck hovers, and turns him
Toward the open silent west.

BUDDHA AT NADIKA

And Buddha came to where the sea
Curled silver-white upon the land,
And murmurs of infinity
Breathed on the sand.

And there lay shells like rosy foam
Borne from the caverns of the deep,
Frail playthings drifted from the home
Of timeless, tideless sleep.

And on the sands a Fisher stood,
Drying his nets that late had seen
The silent caverns of the flood
And all the wastes between.

The Fisher lingered in his place
With countenance of mild surprise,
And looked upon the Buddha's face
With dumb, uncomprehending eyes.

And Buddha spake: "Thy nets are drawn,
Thy boat rocks idle on the sea,
Thy day turns westward and is gone. . . .   ,
Come thou with me."

The Fisher marvelled: "I must toil
With nets and shells among the caves,
To win the sea's unwilling spoil
From the harsh waves."

[205]

And Buddha answered: "Cast no more
Thy nets upon the troubled sea,
Nor gather shells along the shore.
Come thou with me.

"Thou drawest shells and curious flowers
From out the blue untrodden caves—
Thou seest the passing of the hours—
Thou hearest the clamor of the waves—

"Thou openest the shell where lies
The pearl more white than driven spray—
And trackless past thy vision flies
Each passing day.

"But I will teach thee not to stir
The shell nor flower in its sleep.
For thou shalt roam the sepulchre
That chasms all their native deep.

"And vain desire, like terror grown
Deep in the chambers of thy breast,
Shall be from thee forever flown,
And thou shalt rest.

"No search for pearls shall blind thy thought,
Nor waves, with clamorous harmonies.
But in the silence where is naught
Thou shalt behold the One that is.

"And where the days now speed like foam
Across thy vision, there shall be

For thee a vast eternal home—
An Infinite Sea."

The Fisher looked on Buddha dumb—
Looked deep into that tender gaze—
Those eyes within whose depths had come
And gone the sorrows of all days.

He looked uncomprehendingly,
And wearily he shook his head;
And turned once more to drag the sea,
Knowing not what the Buddha said.

Guide to China

The Book of History

In the reign of the great Emperor Lu T'ang Chu,
Wise men were ordered to inscribe in a book
All the vast body of wisdom that men knew . . .
Today I turn the pages, and as I look
I cannot see anything very new or old,
And I wonder why it was worth the trouble, then,
Of days and nights and a thousand labors untold
Which the volume must have exacted from those
    wise men.
But still we write—and the Emperor now is blown
As grey dust over the limitless Asian plains.
Still we inscribe all that is humanly known,
Although no ruler honors us for our pains—
Recording a thousand wisdoms, all our own,
To celebrate our good and glorious reigns.

The Book of Virtue

This is the volume of the Ancient Code,
Each page a sign-post of explicit sense,
Directing up a road or down a road,
And how one journeys thither and how thence,
With notes of dangerous turnpikes. It were well
To sit one down and study out the story—
Grasp the experience that these pages tell
Of saints and sages sin-expert and hoary.
Alas! what pity that our little time
Forbids delay! Relentless toward the west
Moves the high sun out of its tranquil prime;
Relentless shadows close around the breast:
And if our hearts beat out a gipsy rhyme—
Forgive us, prophets, if we think it best!

Local Revolt Against Confucius

There are nobilities of which the name
Stands in dark letters on the roll of shame;
And horrors whose abysm frightens the soul
Lift their bright titles on the honor-roll.
I have known men and women who were good
And also men and women who were evil;
But save when mastered by some Judas-mood
I leave the problem, Which?—all to the devil.
Friends I have had, and enemies: though the first
Gave to me all the sweetness of the heart,
And though the second smote sharp as they durst,
By test of pain I cannot tell them apart.
So, ignorant as a fool, I shall withdraw
From these scenes of the Tables of the Law.

[209]

Tomb of a Late Ming Poet

Once he upraised a clear triumphant voice—
Witnessed the glory of the Primal Cause—
Bade men who suffer forthwith to rejoice—
And gravely took the Emperor's grave applause.
Now bronze and marble testify his worth
That served the noblest in both God and men:
He wrote—"All things on earth are best for earth."
The Emperor marveled, and threw down his pen.
I watched today the solemn delicate fall
Of scattering autumn leaves above his tomb.
The priest said—"This approach of noble gloom
Cannot obscure his greatness, after all."
And in the empty night that followed after
Jangled a great burst of hyena laughter.

Astronomical Calculations from the Ming Observatory

The orbits never fully round, but change
In spiral gropings: not, as on a wall
Flat-patterned—but back into space they fall
In depth on depth of indeterminate range.
Where they begin may be here at my hand
Or there, far-lost beyond the reach of eye.
And though I sit, desperately rapt, and try
To trace round-round the line, and understand
The sequence, the relation, the black art
Of their continuance, hoping to find good
At least some logic of part-joined-to-part,
I judge the task one of too mad a mood,
And cease; and watch the eddies from my heart
Go circling down the currents of my blood.

[210]

Speculations of a Mandarin

Two mirrors, face to face, is all I need
To build a mazy universe for my mind
Where world grows out of world. I dizzily find
Solace in endless planes that there recede.
The fifth plane-world, soft-glimmering through the
      glass,
Surely it has a light more bland than ours.
And in the far ninth hides a whirl of powers
Unknown to our dull senses. I would pass
Down the long vista, pausing now and then
To taste the flavor of each separate sphere
And with each vast perspective cool my eye.
Whom should I meet there? Never living men!
What should I love there? Nothing I hold dear!
Where would the end be? Endless as am I!

All Things Are Their Opposites in China

If there were nothing, nothingness would be
Wiped out of being by that suicide;
And back would bloom the universe that had died,
From death by death's last victory thus set free.
So, lust—whose might enslaves the mortal frame,
Dazing the spirit with vast sensual glooms,—
At its great height of evil power, consumes
The flesh, and bursts in worship and a flame.
So, the proud spirit that on lofty wings
Surveys all mortal life, and comes to know
The world as fields and seas beneath it strown,
At last rejects the sight of earthly things,
So desperate they; and, sailing to and fro,
Is no more spirit, but tired fowl alone.

Secret Instructions for Reaching Xanadu

Go eastward from the Bewildered-Dragon Lake
Until you see the Monastery of the West
Tower straight and high above your head.   Then
        take
Those charms which, as I told you, in the breast
Of your most inner robe you have hidden, and
        follow
Their clear instruction: firstly, you will swim
Like a carp up the cataract; then, as swallow,
Lift yourself out of the foaming whirl and din—
And quite forgetting all you could ever learn
Of man's astronomy, sweep into the east
Of cool and rosy sunrise.   There you must turn
On slow wing-circles till you descry a priest
Deaf, dumb, and blind.   Go to him.   If he think
        best
He will disclose to you how to achieve the rest.

At St. Stephanos

High, high above the thatched roofs of the town,—
An hundred times more high than lifts the tower
Of the Cathedral,—higher than the song
Of nightingale ascends, or swallow's wing—
There, where the splintered cliff dizzily drops,
Sheerer than headland of Gibraltar's straits,
In one precipitous rock-cloven wall
To low-lying fields,—there stands an ancient House
Of refuge and secluded holiness.

   Toward it at sunset from the plains I came,
Through long defiles ascending, past gaunt slopes
And barren gullies of the wind-swept hills
Tenantless as the moon. Upon the crests
The light still shone; though far below, the dusk
Covered the fields, and with the fear of night
Amid these wilds pursuing me, urged on
My climbing feet.

            Suddenly on a crag
That century-beaten, gray-walled monastery
Against the solemn fires of the west
Lifted its battlements and pointed roofs
And faintly smoking chimneys, in the dusk
Bastions of grayness. My approaching step
Echoed upon the drawbridge, whose frail span
Across a narrow deeply-cloven chasm
Hung tremulous. Through the dim portal arch

And low cold passageways of mouldering stone
I passed, in wonder at these massive walls;
And stood in the gray court,—as empty now
As though its vanished centuries had borne
With them away into far gulfs of Time
What life had once found place here. On three
　　sides,
The alcoved galleries of the cloisters rose,
Half-ruined, cheerless: on the fourth, a gate
Out toward a platform opened, where the rock
Became the precipice. There spread the West
A burning flood before me, and the peaks
Of the white Pindus from it rising up
Like snow-capped islands; and far, far below,
Even at my feet, submerged beneath the tide
Of shadowy haze, the plains of Thessaly.

Then in the high still air a bell began
Somewhere its vesper tolling; and those sounds,
Blurring and blending with recurrent strokes,
Drifted about me, islanded aloft
Upon that far-seeing headland; while below,
Small and remote, the villages of the plain
Withdrew into the mists of eventide.
And pausing thus, upon my spirit came
That nameless sense,—like odour in a dream,—
Of ending Summer and the sudden hour
Of the year's passing which September brings
To thrall the musing wanderer on the slopes.
Then the bell ceased; and from the chapel doors
Poured St. Stephanos' holy Brethren forth,
Dark men and bearded, clad in girdled robes,—
The garb of those who from the general band

[214]

Of priesthood had themselves to single life
Vowed, and to poverty,—not the common lot
For clergy of Byzantium. Forth they strode
With kindly faces and the greeting hands
That are the portion of a stranger chanced
From the great world unto monastic walls,—
About whose base the seething tide of days
Beats with tumultuous surges, casting up
To this lone height rarely a drop of spray
Or sound articulate of the dizzy strife.

With friendly cheer, they took my pack and staff;
And led me to the ancient raftered hall
Where, round a board sufficient for the need
Of three-score Brethren, the remaining few,—
Seven and the Abbot,—took their daily fare.
Diminished now that ancient company
Which in the darker ages here maintained
A citadel of peace amid wild wars.
Paler, this band, and of less dominant blood,—
Yet Brethren of great St. Stephanos still,
And heritors of those who once upreared
This lonely fortress for the praise of God.
Strange men, strange heritors, these my hosts to-
        night;
With whom I sat, and ate the evening meal
Of kid and lentils and thin acid wine
With resin steeped,—scant fare, befitting priests
Vowed unto poverty in a meagre land,—
Not milk and honey;—and heard the simple talk
Of the old Abbot,—how the Summer closed
Early this year; and how the long ascent
Had left me weary, doubtless. And this speech

[215]

Of common things which drifted to and fro
Served but to fill me with a keener sense
Of utter strangeness. Round our casual talk
I felt great vistas opening pathless out,—
Unsounded hopes and passions of these hearts,
Alien to mine. From these unfathomed eyes
Looked forth the keepers of a secret life
Upon a separate world, to me unknown.
Their gaze beheld another sun than mine;
The very breeze to them not as to me
Bore waftures of unrest or peace or pain;
Within their souls a different dream of heaven
Sustained or tortured. And that wonder grew
As down the table from grave face to face
My glances strayed; and strong my passion burned
To know what meaning filled their thoughts and
          days,—
What boundaries and what contours marked the
          world
Which, through the strange refraction of the soul,
Each one surveyed, alone.

                    I thought they seemed,—
These Brethren of the Heights,—kind, simple
          hearts,
Rude shepherds of rude flocks, unlettered, slow,
Habituated to the pious days
And narrow duties of the monastery.
Within those eyes no subtler passion leaped
Than dogmas of corporeal heaven and hell
Might teach them: and their little round of being,
Changeless, sufficient, circumscribed and pure,
Passed like the herdsman's in the lowlier plains—

Daylight to dusk, and year to year, one course
Of unreflective tasks that left no trace
Upon the scroll of inward history.

But one among the Brethren, whom the rest
Called Theodorus, seemed of other mould
Than all his fellows. In his face the South
Spoke warm and radiant. Something in his gaze
Like hesitant intensity of fire
That flickered, clung, and died,—or the full lips
And delicate profile, bringing to my mind
A poet of pale beauties, lately dead,
Whom now his land acclaimed,—or the desire
Hardly concealed, which made his features glow
Attentively a listener as I told
Some curious traveller's tale,—these drew my
        thought
Recurrently to him. And when his smile
Gleamed with a flash of eagerness for joy,
Like starlight among candles, then I felt
A sudden pang of pity. Here, I thought,
Was one to whom the lusty sinful world
Was not well lost,—in whom still burned the spark
Of love for all which faith calls vanity.
His face betrayed the harp vibrant within.
The call of beauty never unto him
Were cold, unmeaning. Each mysterious voice
Which from the loveliness of hill or cloud
Or dream or music calls our blood, as calls
The west wind to the waves,—these things would be
For him the secret masters of his soul.
And while his Brethren mounted to Heaven's Gate
With calm unswerving steps, him must the breath

Of Maytide mornings make their quivering sport.
A bird-note could whirl chaos through his prayer.
His avowed allegiance to the Virgin Throne
Must waver at the beauty of a flower
Or the soft curve of some girl's shadowy throat
Seen in the dusk. And if at last he gained
The prophets' Paradise, it needs must be
By hard-won mastery which to ruder souls
Were all unknown. Perilous lay the road,
Through chanting vales, to his celestial home.

At length the meal was ended; and we passed
In straggling twos and threes out of the hall
To the rock-platform, where the stars looked down
Brilliantly on us, and the gulf beneath
Lay vague and fathomless. Beside me paced
Now Theodorus, as in eager talk
He held me from the rest; with outstretched arm
Pointing this place and that,—towns, mountains,
        streams,—
All hidden in the night. And one by one
The Brethren left us for their evening tasks;
He only lingered yet.

                    "Tell me," he said
"How moves the world in Athens? Do they still
Place little tables at the café doors,
And sit all afternoon, and watch the crowds,
And smoke and talk? And do the soldiers drill
Out beyond Lycabettus as they used?
And the Piræus, that bright sinful port,
Do the great ships still crowd the harbor's mouth,

And boatmen throng the wharves?— Or has the
    world
Grown quieter than in my day?

                    "The world,"
I answered, "is not quick to change its ways.
I think that you would find all things the same,
Even to the tables,—where three days ago
I sat and smoked and watched the crowds go by,
And saw the King pass with his shining guards
And troops of cavalry."
                His attentive eyes
Gleamed with the picture.
              "And when did you last
See white-walled Athens?" I with idle thought
Questioned him. And with slow words he replied—
"Twelve years ago: then I became a priest." . . .
And spoke no more; but shortly turned away,
Murmuring of his tasks that must be done.

    Then paced I silently the platform's bounds;
As, on some farthest rampart of the world,
Alone, at night, a spirit from the stars
Beyond Orion might alight and pace;
And looking down upon the sleeping earth
From that secluded outpost's icy height,
Marvel in silence on the pageant spread
Beneath his vision, with the crowded thoughts
Of one whose being had therein no part.
And for this spirit tenanting my breast
Wonder was dominant,—labyrinthine moods,—
And sense not of the kinship of mankind
But of life's strangeness and the infinite forms
Of days and destinies.

                      [219]

The processional stars
Moved slow above me. As I tarried still,
Out of the cloisters Theodorus came
And silently rejoined me; and our steps
Sounded together, back and forth the rock.
The great hush of the hour, the shroud of dark,
Stifling all echoes of departed day,
Enfolded us. We were alone with night,—
Night, that in such a silence seems to drop
The measureless beatings of gigantic wings
On the frail heart. With such a presence close,
Our deep seclusion from the sleeping world,
Our slow concordant footfalls, wove a sense
Of some strange bond between us as we strode
Mute and together. On that barrier-ledge,
Raised like an altar to the lifeless stars,
A magic greater than old fellowship
Drew me to him with whom I seemed alone
In the vast dusk: across the trackless seas
That sunder man from man, my thought reached out
To touch this alien, who for one strange hour
Seemed as a brother.

Something bade me say,
After long silence—"I could half believe
That all the world lay dead beneath our feet,
And you and I upon this lonely rock
Solely remained."

"Sometimes not more alone"
He said, "than thus, is one who strays afar
Circled by minds that have a different birth."
And through the darkness his unquiet eyes
Seemed bent upon me.

[220]

Well I knew he spoke
With thought of me, a stranger; but to me
An alienage profounder than my own
Seemed to encircle him; and to his words
I answered, with his keen impassioned face
Vivid before my sight.—

"My friend," I said,
"For you this pinnacle must be a tomb:
You need the sunlands."

And he understood,
And flushed, with changing eyes, as though my
          words
Had touched the harp-strings in his breast and
          waked
Unutterable voices.

"No," he cried,
"No land,—but life!" . . .

His speech faltered away;
And I could feel beneath the burdened words
An impulse,—rare in our cold northern race,—
The longing to reveal to alien eyes
Things that perhaps could never be revealed
Save to a stranger,—one whose path lay far,
So far that never any later day
Of faith turned bitter could bring forth regret
That he had spoken

But no words I said,
Being unwilling to invite his speech
Unless his heart impelled him; I but drew

[221]

A little closer, with attentive ear:
While ministry of silence told my mood
With greater eloquence than mortal tongue
Could master, doubtless; and I heard his breath,
And tremors seemed to shake him; and at last
From subterranean chambers hid from light,
Long sealed and voiceless, now in broken words,
With many a pause and space for groping thought,
Poured forth a torrent of tumultuous speech
Broken and eloquent, furious and shy.

"I think that you are one who understands.
When our eyes met across the board to-night
You looked at me with glance that well might read
Something of those dim travails of the mind
Which to the Brethren here upon the rock
Possess no being. Righteous men are these,
But peasant-priests, half-kindred to the herds,
Ignorant of the strange convulsive powers
That may inhabit us. . . .

     "My stranger-friend,
Things long repressed burn on my lips to-night,
Born of your look, your voice." . . .

      Gently I said—
"I will devote my heart to understand."
And at those words, he spoke—as Winter snows
In the Spring floods sweep o'er the thirsty lands.—

————

"You find me here, a Brother in the halls
Of St. Stephanos; but my birth was far
In southern islands, where the Cyclades

Lie like a barrier westward from one isle:—
O isle of brightness I shall not know again,
Mykonos, bride of sea-winds and the sea!
My home, amid the windmills on the heights,
Looked out toward Delos and the western waves
Wherein the sun sank down each eventide
With hues that were to me song poured from
        heaven,—
A wild enchantment, drawing forth my soul
In longing for all beauty. On the hills
Of her, my rocky island, as a boy
I walked in vision; and the ancient tales
Of Homer, and the legends of the shrine
That once was crown of Delos, and the forms
And colors and wild odors which my dreams
Wove from the sunsets and the changing spray,
Wrought in my soul a passion, a desire
Past understanding, for exalted deeds
And life that should be beautiful, like the Gods!
I was a Pagan, with the bards who sang
Once from these isles the praises of the fair
Golden Apollo. From some headland rock,
Looking across the waves, I could have raised
My pæan, too, of sacrificial joy
Unto the deities of sun and sea!

   I scarce remember in what forms I dreamed;
Yet well I know that dreams by night and day
Moved where I moved, building a world apart
From unregarded casual daily things.
I dwelt among those moments, few and crowning,
Which chronicle and legend garner up
From the lone triumphs of heroic hearts,—

Time's precious harvest, slowly winnowed forth
Out of the lives of thousands who go down
Barren of such a radiant grain. All peaks
Whence man views life as lord:—what Jason saw
With the first hope, and at the final goal;
What Alexander felt when the last gate
Of secret Eastern city fell, and kings
Knelt at his chariot; what Euripides
Knew as the multitude with bated breath
Quivered and was dumb to hear Electra speak:—
Out of such marvelous fragments as these things
I wrought my fair mosaic, that served my faith
As pattern of the world and of man's life.

Ah, I was happy! but no more content
Than ever man is. My enkindled thoughts,
Fed upon visions, whispered that afar
And yet untasted lay that sunlit world
Whereof the pallid moon-dreams of my youth
Were but a shadow and a prophecy.
Glowing, it called me toward the richer days
Of which my hope breathed and the poets sung.
Now must the mystery, long viewed afar,—
Life, Life itself, unbosom unto me
Its beautiful meaning. Wherefore did I stay,
Tarrying in the porch before the shrine?
Nay, I would enter to the inmost hall,
To the close presence of that deity
Who, though remote, with palpitant glowing touch
Had waked divinest madness in my breast,
And the dim promise of sharp loveliness,
And uttermost longing for the clasp of Life.

[224]

Therefore, obedient to that stirring call
Heard in lone hours, filled with exalted thought,
I left my rocky island and keen spray
Of salty winds, and unto Athens came,
There to abide and earn my bread and find
The undiscovered marvels of my fate.
And can you picture,—you, with thoughtful eyes,—
How in the city fared that dreaming boy,
Credulous still of all the golden tales
Which from the poets' music and the light
Of sunset-wests he had distilled to drops
Of keener essence? Can your vision pierce
The coarse engulfing crowds of teeming men
Down to the last deep, where in shrinking doubt,
I, child and dreamer, moved,—first whelmed by
          power;—
Then lost, as, by some spell, the pomp and stress
Crumbled about me,—and I stood alone
In a vast desert? Dust, pitiful dust
Lay that existence in my shrinking hand.
Where was the lofty doom my dreams had sung?
Where were the ecstasies and the hours of flame?
Bewildered grew the promise of my soul,
As the world's business, sordid oft and base,
Seethed by me like a nightmare: all men's thoughts
Seemed rapt in petty matters which like leaves
Floated upon the vortex of the hour
And then were drowned beneath the on-rushing
          stream,
Forgotten and unmemorable. Those hearts
In whom, I thought, long intercourse of life
Had surely stored some more-revealing sense
Of what our being meant, and what was good,

And where the true goal for our striving lay,—
Those, intricately netted, seemed to dwell
A thousand fathoms deep beneath the tide
Of fragmentary labors toward no end,
Like play of madmen. None, of all I saw,
Felt the great doubts that hem our mortal lot,
Or looked with wonder toward the tranquil stars
Or into the far depths of his own soul.
Unguided conflict,—random ebb and flow
Of days and deeds,—confusion of one force
Smiting against another in its path,—
What could I make of these unreasoned things?
And to my sense, fevered with strange dismay,
Men loomed like brutes who in the forest roved,
Whose history was recorded by gnawed roots
And trampled grasses,—and white bones at last.

   Another race they seemed; yet as I dwelt
There in the town, and labored at my trade
Shoulder to shoulder with them, slowly passed
That sense of alienage. Into my thought
Slowly there entered, gradual bit by bit,
Some consonance with theirs. By painful steps
I came to know why toiling men put by
The visions that had nurtured them in youth.
I saw the vanity of the rootless joy
Which youth and beauty foster till the hour
When weight of burdens kills the fragile bloom.
The harshness of the actual iron world
Broke in upon my spirit. I beheld
Bitter realities as the ruling force
Upon this pitiful soul of ours, which strains
Heavenward on frail wings. I saw the dream,

Woven of all the past's enchanted gold,
Shattered by those necessities which ride
With vast material dominance through the realm
Of spiritual being. I saw earth, sea,
Time, space, all yield, reluctant, to the toil
Of man who in that desperate flux and press
Battles for barely life. Until at last
I, also, cast all hope and rapture by;
Acknowledged me as servant of cruel powers,—
A pigmy struggling in a tragic world
For mere existence:—I, who late had thought
To choose among the destinies of the Gods
For which should best accord with my desire!
Thereupon I became as other men,
Spending my heart upon each worthless task,
Incurious of the meaning; and, as they,
No longer scrupulous of little things
Like careless wrongs, or other lives awry
By my rough passing: I no longer set
Patterns of beauty for the weary soul;
But as of very need, accepted quite
The creed that was my fellows', half-resigned
Unto a world of chaos ultimate.

So the years passed, as in the city's streets
I moved and had my life, where crowded days
Stifled all pause for thought. Yet in the Spring
Sometimes strange passions would revisit me;
And night-long I have lain awake to watch
The bright processions of my former dreams
Arise again and pitifully lead
Their ranks in holy wars to conquer back
The soul's lost empire from those tyrant powers

Which should have subject station and obey,
Not master, life. And lo! one April noon
As at my task I labored, from lone deeps
Long buried in me, burst a fierce revolt
Against that creature which I had become.
I cried—This life of mine, this dull, misshaped
And vegetable being, shall not be
My final sepulcher! I will arise:
I will go up into the lofty places
Apart from all man's works, and there commune
With God and mine own soul. I will search out
By lonely thought some meaning or accord
Or radiant sanction that may justify
The ways of life. The void and troubled world
Will I renounce, to gain in solitude
What the world gave not,—sense of life's design.

Then fared I toward the mountains of the north,
That land behind us yonder, where the wastes
Of aught but God's own self are tenantless.
And wandering aimless, in the weary mood
Of one who finds the glories of the earth
Glamouries only, to this spot I came,—
A far retreat whose name to me was known
Long as a legend. When I saw these walls
Which from their dizzy height looked calmly down
Upon the distant world,—beheld the blue
Of tranquil heaven around these summits cling,
Where no sound broke the silence of the slopes,
Lo! this, I felt, was my abiding-place,
My spiritual home, where life might be
Once more my own and not the multitude's.
Thereupon, with glad zeal, I sought the gate,

[228]

Begging admission to the brotherhood;
Though little holiness was in my soul
Save that which God's omniscient tender eyes
Might find in the wild longing that was mine
For something nobler than my days had found.
And when my rapt novitiate was past,
I with exultant lips assumed the vow
Of life-long service, and irrevocably
Closed the last portals of the world behind.

Peace here I sought, a little peace from life,—
A little time that might pass gently by
Afar from the coarse clamors of the world
And purposeless confusions. I would trace
In silence and seclusion that fine thread
On which are strung, like fair or faded flowers
Along a garland, the successive days:
Which in the city's press become a heap
Of crushed disordered blossoms, and conceal
The filament that joins them. For, I thought
That, as a reveler by cups of wine
Now overcome no longer tastes the grape
But madness only—so where life is swift
And strong and tense and multitudinous
Of forms and deeds, there life annuls itself
Into confusion; and the crowded years
Are filled with living till no life remains.
Hence with great yearning I desired to dwell
Apart from these things, in a place of peace
Where, from the visions of the sunrise hills
And books and musing talk and the low voice
Of my own soul, I might remould the world
Into a pattern beautiful and clear.

My hope was high to reconcile at last
The harsh disorder of the warring earth
With needs and verities that dwelt within. . . .
I try to tell you these things but I think
I cannot pour their meaning into words
Unless you too already somewhat know
Whereof I speak. . . .

                    Slow passed the tranquil days
Of my first years in St. Stephanos' walls.
Prayer, and long service at the altar-place,
And common speech, and silence much alone,
Were mine as portion. But contentment dwelt
No more with me. Great weariness in its place
Became my fellow, and a sense of foiled
Inaction haunted me, more hard to bear
Than turmoil. For the visions came no more
Which once at Mykonos had filled my soul;
Or if they came, of little worth they seemed
To one who had beheld the toiling world
And the great pulsing streams which in the streets
Of crowded cities meet and part and strain
In dim and purgatorial confluence.
Somberly I beheld, with alien eyes,
My brother-priests serve at the altar-cross,
And with untroubled worship send their souls
Straight through the incense to the blissful seat
Of God the Father. But my lagging thoughts
Tarried behind upon the strong young heads
Of the few shepherds who, amid these heights
Now wandering, knelt at mass within our gates.
Their troubled lives, their toil, their fears and hopes
Stood between me and Heaven. Their life was mine,

Their laboring days were mine. I felt arise
Like a great tide the sense of fleeting things—
Tenderness, joy, labor and hope and strife,—
All ours a little while, then to be gone;
But when departed, treasured in the heart
With clinging light of old remembrances.
I felt that glow, unutterably sweet,
Which makes the love of life haunt all our days
With wonder and desire. My homesick breast
Longed for the eager city and its stress
Of meeting man with man :—things theirs, but now
Not mine for evermore. And then, too late,
In certitude I knew myself one born
A passionate child of life and not of dreams.

    As here I dwelt through slow unchanging days,
This knowledge waxed in me. Gone was the hope,
Eternally, I think, of infinite joy
Awaiting in some fortunate golden land.
But the rude fellowship of the eager world
Called me, and calls me still. I am content
With quieter thoughts than those which once trans-
        formed
My being, as the sunlight a fair cloud
Transfuses into wonderful wreaths of gold.
No more do I desire upon the hills
To stand at even, and feel through my veins
Pour wild unutterably stirring breath
Of harmony with some transcendent lyre
Singing where sunset faded down the slopes.
For I have passed the magic of that time
And youth's unbodied visions. I have seen
The half-lights of the exquisite morning fade,

And daylight walk the land. And I have taught
The baffled spirit to forego its dreams,
Content within a less imperial space,
Amid the things that are. For now, I think
That nothing in the world is wholly fair
And nothing wholly foul; but all are blent
Of a strange stuff, whose mingled dark and bright
I saw, and still must cherish till I die.

O youths who stand upon the singing hills,
Your bosoms full of singing! Well you know
The sacred light of vision, the unrest
Of pure desire for some immortal goal!
But you have yet to learn the common face
Of life and days and plain realities
And the slow reconcilements of the heart.

But I have learned; and now I long to go.—
I would return unto the city's strife,
And move amid the vast and thrilling crowds,
Those wonderful crowds of living, breathing men;
And feel again the wildly stirring sense
That every passing form might prove to me
A comrade or a brother or a foe,
A lover or a well of fierce desire!
With unsolved powers each one is eloquent.
There in the city moves no single form
So mean or lofty that it may not be
A shuttle in the dizzying gold-shot web
Which, stretching out on all sides round me there,
Inscrutably is woven; and creates,
Out of chance looks and errant turns and stops
And random meetings and unpurposed words,

The infinite woof that is my life and me.
That life I cry for! Here I die of dreams.
I perish, as a breath along the wastes."

———

And I, to whom the tale had been a scroll
In a strange language writ, which line by line
Revealed dim meaning, could not make reply.
But looking down from those monastic walls,—
That hoary refuge of a thousand years
Remote upon the precipice of the rocks,—
Once more the sense of ending Summer crept
Out of the night upon me: and once more
I seemed as one who looks from a far place
Upon a scene wherein he has no part.
I viewed, as one beholds a gathered flower,
Man's life, and its strange pitifulness; so sweet
That memory makes the heart to overflow:
So bitter that men turn from it, as turned
This soul beside me, to the world of dreams:
So fleeting, that the darkness hovers close
Even while the seeker pauses to debate
The better path, or turns to mourn in vain
A choice regretted, and the days go by
Bearing what still remains. . . .

                         With calmer words
Now Theodorus spoke.—
                         "For I would have
A little light, leaping from eye to eye,—
A little warmth, as hand grasps eager hand
In swift adventure at whose every turn
Some eager lure awaits:—it is not much,

But it is everything! Tenderness, joy
Labor and love and strife,—all fleeting things,
But sweeter than the sharp sweet island wine,
And the one solace . . . and the one solace!"

Then without pause for answer, he was gone
And the night hid him. To my troubled rest
Shortly I went, nor sought his side again,
Having no speech to answer the dim tale
Which he had uttered, though I think he knew
It was not coldness silenced me.

                                        At dawn
I rose and forth proceeded on my way
Over the mountains. As I turned to look
Back for the last time at those old gray walls
And weathered battlements, my final sight
Was Theodorus, in his following eyes
That strange tense wistfulness for joy and life,
As from the gate he waved me a farewell.

The Headland

At the cliff's base he looked up, and there saw her
High on a headland, like a Venus risen
Above the earth to front the eternal skies.
Then madness came upon him. . . .

　　　　　　　　For this land
Was to him wholly alien; he had come
Wandering hither as to the world's last edge
In search of doubtful peace.　Here where the coast
Jutted in cliffs and granite promontories
Over the seas, and took the flooding waters
Into the depths of labyrinthine caves
And weeded estuaries, here he walked
Day after day, a pilgrim whom no shrine
Yet had sufficed.　But in the hardy bloom
Of heather on these hilltops, and in the bleak
Iron frugality of the huts that raised
Their thatches here and there, and in the gleam
Of rigor and resistance in the eyes
Of the few peasants, he caught sometimes sense
Of a strong bitterness that might save his soul.

Today with knapsack and half-blunted staff
He had again set out along the shore,

Traversing sometimes the wide sands of bays
And sometimes scaling boulders where the crags
Had cast their wild detritus down to sea.
"Down from the heights," he thought, "the great
    crags molder
In the assault of each indifferent year—
Heights like the ones that once within my spirit
Lifted their splendid precipice to confront
All stars and seas—where now the incessant years
Gnaw rock to drifting sand. What now remains
Is shamed by loftiness of these strong walls—
Walls strong as yet, though even now while I watch
I know them moldering seaward as do I.

   "So speaks this land to me,—this granite and
    iron,—
Of tragic fortune; yet in its defeat
Braced to resistance, nerved to high disaster
And an eternal sternness. Thus alone
With stoic hardness must the hills confront
Sky and the stars when all their flowers are gone
Under the sea-wind.

                "Vanishing flower-world! . . .
Men toil and fight, love and contrive and dream,
And for a little while the mad illusion
Holds them. And then the beauty sickens away
Beneath the irony of the mortal fate,
Today's fate and tomorrow's.—Till in the end
They must go down to the edge of the waste sea
And walk alone as I now walk alone. . . ."
    [236]

Then at the cliff's base, suddenly looking up
He saw upon the headland high above him
A woman's form. Her clear and upturned head
Fronted the ocean-plain: her streaming hair
Tossed in the sea-wind: in one drooping hand
Some snowy garment fluttered as she stood
Naked, sublime, exultant in the sun
Drinking the lonely spaces. To her feet
Rose up the tawny bastion of the rock,
Scarred as by fires of ancient conflagration,
Higher than any sea-gull's questing flight
Above the low shore-levels; and beyond her
In an unclouded majesty of light
Trembled the deep blue of the summer sky.

And he at this mirage stood staring up
Incredulous. Then as her beauty mixed
With the sky's beauty and the rocks' and the sea's
Within his heart, a swift tumultuous sense
Of joyfulness swept through him; he remembered
Suddenly songs that he had long forgotten,
And youthful dreams in moonlight-haunted fields
And futile faiths that once had mastered him
In Autumn dusks. Out of these buried deeps
Now to the light stormed phantoms long-imprisoned
By bitter walls,—a flash of the world's beauty
And a wild cry for happiness. There she stood,
Image of joy, a shout and a revelation.
Glory! Glory! Glory! Youth and the sun,
Life in its royal hour, there lifted up
A pinnacle toward the sky; doubting and dust
Fell from him, as the triumphant leap of Summer
Here touched fulfillment.

Well he knew that she
Also, like the great cliffs, must crumble down
Slowly to formless clay: her proud young body
Must some day too yield to the lapping waves
Of time around her feet. But for this hour
She faced the sun, lordliest being of earth,
White and all-conquering. And her call rang out
Across the waves like the call of a silver trumpet
Fierce in his ears. He lifted his head in pride,
Once more awakened to the stirring charge
Of desperate living—once more marching forth
In the glad army to assault the dark
With torches of desire.

    Then out of shadows
His spirit toward the sun-lands sent its cry:
"There is a wonder, still, keen in the world—
There is a splendor still—and on that height
Perhaps I shall achieve it. There, with the sea
Sending its mighty pulses up to us
Perhaps we shall know each other like gods on peaks
Of some lost star—there we shall be at last
Victorious and transfigured—rush together
Like grappling planets in the void, and be
For one hour, bloom of the world,—for one hour,
  crown
Of the dim years of failure!"

    And thereafter,
As though he were lifted by the winds of the sea
Or the winds of his own spirit, he sprang up
Toward the great cliff's base, and with quivering
  steps

[238]

Clambered from rock to rock. The iron front
Of the sheer wall obeyed him, as his dream
Drove him upward and upward. Dizzily below
Grew the long space; but never looking back
He set his passion toward the brow of the cliff.
The sharp-edged granite gnawed his clawing fingers·
And as his feet slipped, he more fiercely clung
And climbed and strove on irresistibly.
His heart beat riotously; his soul with song
Seemed shouting out his triumph, lost and shaken
With winds of heroic battle,—mad and crying
Its flaming hymn of gratitude to have found
A wonder worth its passion of desire.

And slowly came the cliff's edge into view
High over him; then nearer; then he paused,
And with the deep breath of a swimmer plunging
Through a vast wave, he slowly raised himself
Up the last height,—and there, across the edge
Of the brink, grew into sight the woman he sought.

Unconscious on the windy brink she stood,
Her head poised motionless, fronting up and out
Over the winds and waters. Her loosed hair
Would have been dark in cities, but here burned
Into a flame of deep dull-surfaced gold
Like dagger-handles from Etruscan tombs
Or smoldering poppies. A wide generous light
Across her brows swept,—light that grandly spreads
Down lands of gradual valleys where the corn
And wine of the rich year ripens in silence.
Her eyes looked out wonderfully over-sea,
Quiet, emptied of meaning, now made one

[239]

With the vastness that they gazed on; and her lips
Stirred not, but waited, parting as though a smile
Of mighty gladness sometime there should come.

Then he, a little rising, step by step,
Beheld her throat, columned in slender strength,
That blent with powerful benignant shoulders
Of ancient statues, and the generous arms
Fitted for work of days or for the shelter
Of man's exhausted sleep.   And from her throat
Slowly sloped the forward-swelling arc
In a proud dominance, smoothly, tranquilly,
Until its even mastery changed and broke
Into divided rondure, and reluctant
Trembled into new drooping curves of song.
And the long lines in echoing course swept downward
To meet the passionate strong springing contours
Of the carved thighs, that might have frozen to
      marble
Save for the quivering light that played across them.
And over the quiet valleys of her body
The living shadows slept as hurricanes sleep.

He poised in dreaming madness. . . .

                              Then she turned
Slowly, unconsciously—till her sudden eyes
Flashed into knowledge—she drew back and shiv-
      ered,
And clutched her arms to her body, dumb and
      shamed.—
And he, poising upon that perilous edge,
Drunk with the dream of an immortal beauty

And a brief splendor of deathless joy, cried out—
"I too have heard the wind-call; I too am here,
Beautiful lover! We on the heights of the world
Meet, that the earth may blossom! this is the hour!"

And the bewildered fear grew in her face
From which the timeless womanhood had fallen
Leaving her but a girl. The triumphant head
Seemed drooping down now to the shaken breast—
The tremulous body paled; the light went out
That had filled her eyes. And he cried—"Beautiful
    one!
Laugh! It has come."

                    She sank to the brown rock
And with a last look of bewildered shame
And weakness, hid her face in her quivering hands.

He saw the light go out,—saw the proud form
Crumble into a sobbing heap,—aware
That the sky darkened suddenly and the glow
Of the golden sun was vanished from the world.
Then his numbed fingers on the granite boulders
Slipped with a dull reluctance; and as they slipped
His heaven-soaring mind evoked once more
The wild and windy vision of the white woman
Against the fathomless blue of the blue sky,—
The light, the dream, the earth's transfiguration.—
As his frail body dashed from rock to rock.